SHOCKER
HANDBOOK

WSU™

Stories, Stats and Stuff
About Wichita State Sports

By Kirk Seminoff

Printed in the United States of America by
Mennonite Press, Inc.

ISBN 1-880652-47-1

PHOTO CREDITS Many photographs, including
almost all shots prior to 1950, come from the
files of the Wichita State Sports Information
Office. The photo on page 117 was provided
by the Special Collections department of
WSU's Ablah Library. All other photos are
from the files of the Wichita Eagle.

ACKNOWLEDGEMENTS

It's one of those decisions that shape the course of your life. Here I was, a ninth-grader at Brooks Junior High, with an excruciating choice: Take an F in English or see "The Battle of New Orleans" in person.

OK, so it wasn't a tough choice. I missed my English class' drama production to wear black-and-gold overalls in the Superdome.

I've been a follower of Wichita State sports since I was old enough to watch Terry Benton rip down rebound after rebound. My Biddy Basketball jersey was Cheese Johnson's 31, and my Little League baseball number was Joe Carter's 30.

So that's why this book has been a treat to work on. I thought I knew a lot about Shocker sports before starting, but this research has opened my eyes to tons of interesting stuff.

Much of the information in the book comes from the files of the WSU sports information office, the university's Ablah Library Special Collections department and research from The Wichita Eagle and the Sunflower.

Many thanks go to Larry Rankin, Ron Burnett and Robin Matz at sports information. They opened their files to me at anytime, including many long hours in what I affectionately call "The Dungeon": An old concession stand in Levitt Arena with mountains of boxes, old trophies and file cabinets with no comfortable seats and a low ceiling that continually put a hurt on this 6-foot-5 frame.

Finally, thanks to Pete Steinert, who edited the book and probably chuckled every time he read of a Michigan basketball victory over WSU. And thanks to Jeff Pulaski, who did a great job with the layout.

By the way, my ninth-grade classmates tell me the play went great. The next Monday, I showed up at school wearing an "I Was There" T-shirt with the 66-65 score on the back. My teacher said she hoped the trip was worth an F.

Oh, Ms. Clark, if you only knew.

For Kim, who has always been there with support, and mom, for raising me on the front row.
– K.S.

INTRODUCTION

If you're a Shocker fan, you know exactly where you were when Greg Brummett jumped into Eric Wedge's arms. Or when Mike Jones took the shot.

Or when you heard that the plane went down.

For thousands of Wichitans over the year, athletics at the university on the hill in northeast Wichita has meant so much. From Fairmount College to the University of Wichita and finally Wichita State, they've roared when Dave Stallworth sank another shot, Joe Carter hit another one over the fence, or Prince McJunkins eluded five, six, seven men for a touchdown.

Wichita is the heart of Shocker Country, and the Shocker Handbook is meant to bring a slice of it to the reader.

The book is broken up into four chapters: men's basketball, baseball, football and, frankly, everything else. That's not meant to slight any of WSU's other successful programs. But the university, and the city, have always thrived on the Big Three. When football struggled, the city struggled to keep it alive. When the Shocker basketball team won on Saturday night, it was that much easier to wake up on Sunday. And when Gene and the Boys won another game, well, all was normal.

The Shocker Handbook isn't meant to be read in one sitting. Flip through it a few pages at a time. There's no hurry. My hope is that if you're a Shocker fan, you'll learn some things you didn't know about Wichita State athletics. If you're not a Shocker fan, well, maybe you'll get a feeling for what so many Wichitans have lived and died over for decades.

Enjoy.

Kirk

TABLE OF CONTENTS

Basketball

It's a cold January night, the kind where smart people venture out of the house only far enough to get another log for the fireplace. But this is game night, and the Roundhouse is heating up.

People brave the chill with tickets in hand, wanting to see their Shockers win another game. They go to see Dave Stallworth have a great shooting night, or Antoine Carr slam down a handful of thunder dunks, or Xavier McDaniel complete another 20-rebound game.

This is Shocker basketball. Ralph, Cleo, The Rave, Big Mo, Cheese, Antoine, Good News, X, Aubrey, and the Roundhouse.

There are other teams at the university and around Wichita, but there's no fever like Shocker basketball fever when the team is doing well. They talk about it in the barber shop, at the bowling alley, on the talk shows, and at every meal of the day.

"Think we can beat Tulsa?" "Who's better, Stallworth or McDaniel?" "Suppose there any tickets left for tonight?"

That's why fans head to their favorite meeting place, at 21st and Hillside. It's THE happening. And once the game is over, they bundle up, trudge through the snow, warm up their cars and head home.

The Shockers won again.

The first men's basketball team at Fairmount College. Front row, Claude Davis, Lawrence Abbey, Walter Martin. Back row, Bliss Isley, Percy Bates, Elmer Cook.

'AND BRING SOMEONE WITH YOU'

The growth in men's basketball at the university didn't come from deep within its roots. Basketball at Fairmount College was almost an afterthought late in 1905. Football was beginning to win consistently, and baseball and track certainly received the bulk of attention once the weather warmed up in the spring.

Tryouts were called late in the fall semester by Willis Bates, a physical training teacher at the college. He wrote in the Sunflower, "Everybody come out with the intention of being the star on the team. Come and bring someone with you."

Plenty of young men showed up for workouts, but many didn't have any idea how to play winning basketball. After all, the sport was only 14 years old and hadn't reached any kind of popularity in the Wichita area.

But with standouts Lawrence Abbey at guard and Percy Bates at center – he was the tallest player at 5-foot-11 – Fairmount won 2 of 6 games in 1905-06. Both wins, over Mulvane High and the Hutchinson YMCA, were played in the basement of the college building.

The worst moments came at the beginning and end of the season: Washburn beat Fairmount 37-10 in the opener, 66-9 in the finale. But as the Sunflower noted about the Fairmount players: "If you had talked to some of them two weeks before the game about basket ball, some probably would have told you they had never seen a game."

A season ticket for the 1910-11 season cost a whopping $1.50, or 15 cents a game.

SHAKY START The first-ever game, against Washburn, was played in the Fairmount basement. Later that night, the Washburn squad traveled across the Arkansas River and beat Friends University.

The Wichita Eagle took note of Fairmount's inexperienced players: "They have had only a few days practice but in that time they have developed a very fair team." And this: "Percy Bates, while showing some ignorance of the fine points of the game. … "

INDOOR FOOTBALL Notice how basketball shorts have often fallen below the knees of some players lately? Well, that's nothing compared to the first Fairmount basketball uniforms. Wearing short-sleeve jerseys, the earliest Shockers wore padded pants that came down over the knees and socks.

DANDY GYM IDEA Following a 47-point loss at Southwestern College in Winfield on Jan. 18, 1908, the Fairmount athletic association pondered the idea of building a school gym similar to Southwestern's. Students thought it was such a good idea that $740 was

Following Willis Bates' departure, Fairmount's players coached themselves in 1908-09. Leading scorer Jay Plank was the captain.

raised in the first 15 minutes of fund-raising. After four days, they had $1,500, and eventually $2,500 in student money was collected. After the gym was constructed, the new building rules appeared in the Sunflower. No. 5 read: "Thou shalt use no slang stronger than 'Darn' when making a play that is a bum."

MAY I HAVE THIS DANCE? Southwestern College liked its gymnasium so much, it wouldn't allow the local YMCA team to play its games there. So on Feb. 18, 1910, Fairmount journeyed to Winfield to play the Y men in the town's dance hall.

Only one problem: It was so slippery, even the best shoes couldn't grip the floor. So players from both teams took off their shoes and socks and played in bare feet. To get better traction, the men would wet their feet, then stamp them in a pile of chalkdust.

By the way, Fairmount's all-time record in barefoot games is 0-1. The Winfield YMCA won 31-25.

FULL-COURT FOLLIES Fairmount's first game with the University of Kansas was actually with the Jayhawks' "B" team, in 1911. The game was played at KU's Robinson Gymnasium, a 4-year-old facility that had the Wheatshockers gawking. Noted the Sunflower, the floor was so big that "guards had to wear opera glasses to see the basket." It's tough to play with opera glasses; KU's JV won 29-6.

HEAVE THE HIGH HOPES Fairmount had its first winning season in 1910-11, going 7-6. So expectations were running high for the next season … when the Shockers won just 2 of 10. Both wins were over Cooper College (now Sterling), and though the first victory came just three games into the season, the Sunflower couldn't hide its frustration: "AT LAST, AT LAST, AH," quipped the headline.

One of those losses was to Southwestern by a score of 54-24. Incredibly, that came after Fairmount led 21-20 at halftime.

BUCK'S BUNCH It wasn't until 1915-16 that Fairmount truly had a strong team. In Harry Buck's second and final season, his troops won seven straight to start the schedule and finished 10-5. Strong Hinman, Earl "Biggy" Mann and Dick Miller were the stars. The Sunflower described the practices as being "but a little rougher, faster and deadlier than the Friends football game last Thanksgiving Day."

SHH, WE'RE THE SHOCKERS Lamar Hoover took over for Buck in 1916 and immediately understated everything.

He told the Sunflower that he was a low-key coach who "didn't want to be handicapped by having a great reputation to uphold." That wasn't a problem; Hoover was 5-21 in two years at Fairmount, though he did come back for another two-year stint in the early '20s and compiled a 25-11 mark.

FRIENDS, FRIENDS? A bitter rivalry that was built on the football field also grew on the basketball floor. In the 1918-19 season, Friends twice beat Fairmount. After the first victory, 38-33, students from both schools threw eggs and bricks at each other, though nobody was hurt.

That night, though, Friends students invaded the Fairmount campus and painted sidewalks, steps and administration building windows with the letters "FU." The bit of mischief broke a truce the schools had struck two years earlier, noted the Sunflower: "Sage diplomats flinched under the staggering realization that the treaty of 1917 had been treated as a scrap of paper."

The presidents of both schools discussed the matter and Friends students were quickly sent to the east side to clean up the mess. Three Fairmount students were also believed to have been kidnapped during the raid, but it was later determined that they had simply stayed overnight at the home of one of the boys.

THE 'UNHOLY THREE' Fairmount started strong in the 1920s, winning 41 games and losing only 13 in three seasons. But Shocker basketball really began to take off by the mid-'20s, when three future Shocker Hall of Famers took the court.

Ross McBurney was WU's first All-American in basketball.

Harold "Buddy" Reynolds and Harold Davis were star forwards and a year ahead of Ross McBurney, the big center from Wichita High School who was a national All-American in high school when WHS won the '25 national championship.

Together, the three helped Wichita to a 19-2 record in 1926-27, still the school's best winning percentage for a season. The Shockers won eight straight, lost to Pittsburg (Reynolds was ill and didn't make the trip), then reeled off another 10 wins in a row. By the time WU lost again, it was in the semifinals of the national Amateur Athletic Union tournament in Kansas City.

ROSS THE BOSS At 6-foot-5, McBurney excelled not only at scoring and rebounding, but passing as well. Setting up in the post, McBurney would take a pass from a guard and distribute it to an open teammate for an easy shot. If the shot was missed, McBurney was often there to tap it back in. The Wichita Eagle called him "easily the best center seen here and so well known as to need no further comment."

STUMBLING ONTO THE FUTURE

In 1928, a 26-year-old coach from Pratt High left his job to come to the big city, to coach the Shockers. Little did Gene Johnson know the success he would enjoy over the next five seasons. Winning 74 games compared to only 24 losses, Johnson is the university's winningest coach of anyone to stay more than three seasons.

But Johnson certainly didn't stop there. In the 1930s, AAU basketball was just as competitive as the college game and it certainly paid better. So Johnson moved on – "Wichita cut my salary twice, so I went," he later told The Wichita Eagle – and coached the Wichita Henrys to three AAU titles. He also took the 1936 Globe Refinery team to the AAU title, and later coached the same bunch as part of the U.S. Olympic team that won the first basketball gold medal at the '36 Berlin games.

The man could coach.

FIGHTING SPIRIT Johnson's first team went 16-6, including a tough 26-25 victory at Fort Hays State. On the way back, there was trouble. "Anyone who thinks the Shockers lack fight should have witnessed a little incident between members of Wichita's quintet and some residents of Hays," wrote Sunflower columnist A.R. McClintock.

"It seems that some truck drivers were somewhat 'lickered up' and were also pugilistically inclined. One of them swung a tire pump at Moffat, who promptly ducked and sunk a counter. It is thought that said trucker's mouth is still bleeding. Even our docile McBurney took a hand in the proceedings and eyewitnesses to the brawl say that Mac made a pass at one of the bruisers.

"Such is life in the far west."

In 1929, Ross McBurney joined three former Shockers on the Wichita Henrys, which lost in the AAU finals.

BORDER WARS WU opened Johnson's second season with a home game against Fal YMCA, a team of all-stars from Mexico City. Wichita won easily 41-27, but the Mexicans were so impressed by the Shockers' sportsmanship and style of play that their delegation invited the WU clan to tour Mexico after the season.

Two years later, the trip was made. WU won all eight of its games, but that wasn't even close to the best thing that happened on the trip.

ON THE OTHER HAND There were some down sides to the trip, too. WU made the Mexico adventure three straight seasons, but '33 may have been the most memorable.

Among the headaches: The players' clothes were stolen in San Antonio; one of the team's cars supposedly had to be pushed 30 miles after a broken gas line; waiting four hours for help to fix a flat (their jack was stolen,

'LOST IN THE SHUFFLE OF HISTORY'

Between flat tires, stolen clothes and cases of diarrhea during their Mexico journeys, the University of Wichita basketball teams learned more on the basketball court than on sight-seeing tours.

And no one was studying harder than Coach Gene Johnson. WU won most of its games in three years of Mexican tours, but that's only because the Shockers were more talented. The Mexicans, though, had come up with a new innovation.

"They chased us all over the floor and upset us so badly," Johnson later told The Wichita Eagle-Beacon. "I said, 'If a bunch of punks like those Mexicans can drive us crazy doing that, what can we do if we adapt it with some safety measures?' "

A couple of adjustments later and Johnson had pioneered the game of basketball as we know it today. Hardly a college game goes by on ESPN that some team isn't employing full-court defensive pressure.

Today, they call it good defense. In the '30s, they called it

Gene Johnson

"fire department" basketball and labeled Johnson "a renegade."

But the pressure, most often used in a 2-2-1 zone press, always worked. Using it in Johnson's last season at WU, the Shockers went 14-2. Johnson also coached AAU national champions and was coach of the first Olympic basketball champions at Berlin in 1936.

While noted Hall of Fame coaches such as Kansas' Phog Allen and Oklahoma A&M's Hank Iba were perfecting their half-court games, Johnson took the game into a new era.

"I watch basketball on television and I feel proud," Johnson said three years before his death in 1989. "I sort of feel like I invented the modern game."

but they bought the exact one back the next day at a garage). Said standout player Robert "Red" Shadoan: "Even though our clothes were stolen, I wouldn't trade this trip for anything in the world."

MEANWHILE, BACK HOME WU had more good times under Johnson between Mexico trips. The 1930-31 team was 18-5 and won the Southwestern Intercollegiate postseason tournament, and the '31-32 team was 12-7. Team captain Bill Hennigh and Francis Johnson (Gene's brother) both would become WSU Hall of Famers.

But the 1932-33 squad was Gene Johnson's best. The Shockers lost just two games, winning 14 and playing a new brand of basketball learned on the previous year's Mexico trip. Opposing coaches hated Johnson's 2-2-1 zone press, saying it wasn't even basketball.

No, it was winning basketball.

Francis Johnson joined his brother and coach, Gene, to help WU build a basketball foundation.

Red Shadoan enjoyed conversations during the game.

WU played in an industrial league in 1933-34 because the university was suspended by the North Central Association of Colleges and Secondary Schools.

1. What teams have been WSU's easiest and toughest foes?

2. How much did Ralph Miller make in his first season at WU?

GO, RED, GO Shadoan, a multi-sport Shocker who also has a spot in the school Hall of Fame, was a bit of a celebrity among fans. The Sunflower reported that "Red likes to swap pretty compliments with Shebas on the ringside in between shots – Oh, for a head of red hair and you can't go wrong!"

TRANSITIONAL TIMES The next 17 seasons weren't often kind to the Shockers. There were four winning seasons, but no outstanding teams. Five coaches came and went. Wichita joined the Missouri Valley Conference in 1945-46, finishing a strong second in its first season, but then never breaking into the top half of the standings for another five years.

Then, one spring day in 1951, WU president Harry Corbin placed a call to a Wichita high school coach.

WICHITA HITS THE BIG TIME

Ralph Miller was already a big name in Kansas athletics. As a schoolboy in Chanute, he was a phenomenal basketball scorer (hitting a record 83 points in four state tournament games), a record-setting hurdler and a standout quarterback.

Then, while at Kansas, he set passing records which still stand and was twice a first-team all-conference basketball player. Wichita fans knew him well, as Miller scored 30 of KU's 56 points in a 1942 win over the Shockers at the Forum. It was a KU and Forum scoring record.

Miller's reputation as a winner followed him to the sidelines, too. He was 68-17 in four years at Wichita East, winning the '51 state title. That's when Corbin made the call that would change the face of Shocker athletics for the next 40 years and beyond.

No longer was Wichita a football school that played basketball in the winter. It was basketball first. Always.

WELCOME, SORT OF Miller's hiring was not without controversy. Coach Ken Gunning claimed he was forced out by the university, and athletic director and football coach Jim Trimble resigned because he thought Corbin went over Trimble's head to hire Miller.

But Corbin believed Miller was the one who could turn Shocker basketball into something big. The season before Miller arrived, WU sold nine season tickets in the downtown Forum.

QUALITY PRODUCTS SELL Season tickets went up in 1951 before the Shockers ever played a game. Not only was Miller the new coach, but he brought one of the city's best-ever high school players along with him from East.

Cleo Littleton was the star of the Blue Aces' team that won the '51 state championship, averaging almost 25 points. He originally thought about attending Kansas, but when Miller accepted the WU job, he followed because he thought he could learn more about basketball.

Fans and opponents soon learned plenty about Cleo Littleton.

SMOKIN' SHOCKS Miller's opening game as WU coach was a 62-55 loss at Colorado, but the Shockers soon got the hometown fans stirred up with a 93-59 win over Baylor three days later. The 93 points were a school record … that lasted a day. WU lit up Creighton 100-63 the next night.

It was a sign of things to come under Miller. The Shockers resembled Gene Johnson's final WU team in 1932-33, pressing at every opportunity and employing a fast-break style that still hadn't caught on throughout the country.

THE McKEESPORT PIPELINE What started as an innocent recommendation of a basketball player turned into quite a find for Miller and the Shockers in the 1950s.

Two football players from McKeesport, Pa., came to Miller and said they had a friend back in McKeesport, Jim McNerney, who was a good basketball player. After some initial skepticism, McNerney arrived in Wichita and Miller liked what he saw and gave McNerney a scholarship.

McNerney was a good player, but the relationship Miller developed with McKeesport coach Neenie Campbell lasted a long time. Ron Heller, who had not played high school ball but came highly recommended, averaged 17.4 points in 1960-61, and Lanny Van Eman came from Pennsylvania and was a mainstay of WU squads in the late '50s and early '60s.

Ralph Miller (front) poses with seven of his 1951 recruits: Tom Pomranky, Cleo Littleton, Verlyn Anderson, Ken Schlup, Dale Walker, Bill Keller and Charley Gill.

In Cleo Littleton's first season, Houston agreed to play both of its games in Wichita since blacks weren't allowed to play in Houston.

Despite Cleo Littleton's 18.5-point average, Wichita was 11-19 in Ralph Miller's first season. It was Miller's only losing record at Wichita.

CRAVING MORE After a better 16-11 record in 1952-53, the Shockers had extremely high hopes for 1953-54. Littleton was back for another superb season, as were McNerney, Paul Scheer, senior Gary Thompson and promising sophomore Bob Hodgson.

WU won two of its first three, then reeled off a 14-

THE SHOCKERS' FIRST STAR

He was a 6-foot-3 player who could slash to the basket or shoot it from outside, playing any position on the court. Cleo Littleton, the first Shocker player of national prominence, could do it all. Numbers don't do him justice, but chew on these anyway:

■ Littleton scored a record 2,164 points in a four-year career, averaging 19.0 points.

■ He was the first player west of the Mississippi to score 2,000 points and the seventh overall.

■ Because freshmen were allowed to play in 1951-52 when the Korean War was taking numbers away from the college game, Littleton became the first Missouri Valley Conference player to earn first-team all-conference honors four consecutive seasons.

■ His 18.5-point average as a freshman is easily a Shocker record.

■ He shot 74 percent from the line for his career, including a 22-of-23 game at Houston in 1955.

■ He's one of four WSU All-Americans, but the only one to earn first-team honors in two different seasons.

■ His No. 13 is one of only four numbers retired.

■ Forty years after his last game, Littleton still holds seven WSU records.

Finally, consider all that happened while Littleton was one of the first black players to compete in the Valley. He could not play in some cities, had to stay with black families in others, and many times had sandwiches brought out to him in the bus after his white teammates ate inside.

"Fans were very, very negative about me playing," Littleton once said. "It continued throughout my career. They would always have some kind of racial remark."

Too bad they couldn't look past color and see maybe the finest basketball player Wichita has ever produced.

Cleo Littleton poses for history after scoring his 2,000th point. He would end up with 2,164.

game winning streak that is still a school record. Losses later at St. Louis and to Oklahoma A&M in a jam-packed Forum were the only blemishes on the Shockers' record when WU traveled to Stillwater, Okla., for a key MVC tilt with the Aggies.

Bob Hodgson came from tiny Scammon, Kan., and was WU's big man for the strong teams of the mid-'50s.

COW-POKIN' Wichita had never beaten a Henry Iba team in Gallagher Hall, and the 1954 game was going to be as tough. The Aggies were unbeaten in the conference with three games to play, though WU was 7-2 itself.

WU trailed with seconds remaining, until Thompson stole the ball from A&M's Freddie Babb. Thompson passed to Scheer, who made a jump shot from the corner at the buzzer for a 67-66 victory.

A&M won its last two Valley games, though, clinching the title. But WU already knew its postseason fate.

NIT-PICKING Wichita had already accepted a bid to the National Invitation Tournament in New York. Back then, the NIT was just as prestigous as the NCAA Tournament.

But the Shockers ran into a buzzsaw by the name of Al Bianchi. A future NBA star, he led Bowling Green to an 88-84 victory. The game wasn't as close as the score looked. WU was behind the entire game, yet still finished its finest season 27-4.

Six members of the WU squad feed the pigeons in Time Square during the Shockers' stay at the 1954 NIT in New York.

The 1953-54 team, led by Cleo Littleton (13) and Paul Scheer (3), won a school-record 27 games.

Littleton scored 30 points four times his senior season.

SORRY, FELLAS How valuable was a WU ticket for Littleton's senior season? Cherished enough that the 3,800-seat Forum was so packed, it couldn't accommodate every request for a press pass. Sports Information Director Pat Quinn wrote this note on the front of that year's media guide:

"About tickets, comps, passes or whatever you call them, well, there tain't none of them this winter. Every seat, nook and cranny of the Forum has been sold out since last March."

Don't worry, scribes. A solution was on the way.

PINKIES OUT, EVERYONE Miller took one of his Shocker traditions from his days at KU. Playing for legendary coach Phog Allen, Allen insisted that his players have nothing to eat before games except hot tea, toast and fruit.

That worked well for the Shockers, too, until the 1954 All-College Tournament in Oklahoma City. As WU sat in the OCU dormitory with their usual pre-game meal, the University of San Francisco players exited the cafeteria with fried chicken, steaks, pie and milk.

San Francisco beat WU 94-75 that night and the pre-game menu was tossed. As Miller wrote in his 1990 book "Spanning the Game:" "After all, Cleo Littleton … always liked to have two chili dogs and two colas before a game. Who was I to argue?"

RAISING THE ROUNDHOUSE

The memories are endless. Dave Stallworth being carried out on fans' shoulders after bringing WU back against No. 1 Cincinnati. Ralph Miller sitting on his little stool with his chin resting on his hand. Cliff Levingston, pumping himself up by staring at the opponent's basket just before tipoff. Randy Smithson falling backward after hitting a big free throw against Iowa, capping an afternoon when 11,000 fans' voices seemingly carried their boys in black.

And Stallworth, standing alone at the free-throw line during introductions before his final game.

The Roundhouse has seen a lot.

But in some minds back in 1954, the big ol' flying saucer sitting at 21st and Hillside was never really necessary. "Miller's Folly," some called it. But by that time, to be honest, WU basketball had outgrown the 3,800-seat Forum in downtown Wichita. There was a waiting list for tickets, and it was obvious to most that with a coach like Ralph Miller and players such as Cleo Littleton, a larger arena was needed.

So up went the Roundhouse. Built in just over a year for $1.4 million, the arena was quickly hailed as one of

*The Shockers
in Levitt Arena
Through 1994-95*

*Overall:
433-145, .749*

*When ranked:
74-11, .870*

*Opponent ranked:
40-41, .493*

*Ranked vs. ranked:
13-3, .813*

The WU Fieldhouse, later renamed Henry Levitt Arena, was a state-of-the-art facility when dedicated in 1955.

the premier basketball facilities in the country. In the 1995-96 season, the 5 millionth fan is expected to have his or her ticket torn.

Forty years ago, it was a state-of-the-art home. The circular design, which meant more good seats and fans closer to the action, was quickly copied by other universities. You won't see many new ones like it, though, because the cookie-cutter arenas of today are trying to pack as many seats as possible.

Speaking of which: When the arena was under construction, WU officials were told that it would cost $125,000 to raise the roof enough to put in a balcony for anywhere from 7,000 to 8,000 more seats. The university nixed that idea. During the early 1980s, when Shocker basketball hit another fever pitch, they tossed around the "Raise the Roof" idea again – this time for $13 million.

"Wichita built a wonderful fieldhouse here, but they made it too small," Kansas' Phog Allen said after his Jayhawks played game No. 2 in the new place in December 1955. "They built for the present instead of the future."

BIG O'S BIG NIGHT Wichita's 1957-58 team finished 14-12, but it was a squad with no real star. Four players averaged double figures that season, with center Ev

Cincinnati's Oscar Robertson, guarded here by Al Tate, holds the Levitt Arena record for points in a game with 50 in 1958.

Wessel just a hair shy of 10. The Shockers, who had been ranked in the lower part of the Top 20 for part of the season, were 1-3 against ranked teams when No. 3 Cincinnati visited the Roundhouse on March 1, 1958.

That's when Oscar Robertson put on a show that has yet to be duplicated. Robertson scored 50 points that night, still an arena record. WU hung tough but l ost 86-82, meaning Robertson scored 58 percent of the Bearcats' points.

FINISHING THE FIFTIES They weren't exactly lean times, but the late '50s produced some of Miller's more mediocre teams. From 1955 to 1960, the Shockers never finished much above .500 in the conference nor overall.

There were some pretty good players, though. Guard Joe Stevens, a North High product, became the school's No. 2 scorer behind Littleton with 1,295 points. Al Tate was a high-scoring forward from Coffeyville who also chipped in 10 rebounds a game.

But the 1960s quickly brought new heights to the Roundhouse.

THE FOUNDATION The 1960-61 team went 18-8, by far the best season since Littleton left WU. That Shocker squad had all five starters average double figures, a feat that would be equaled only once more in the next 35 years.

But the groundwork for the Shocker success of the early '60s actually began in the late '50s. Among the infusion of talent were Lanny Van Eman and Ron Heller from Pennsylvania, and a 6-foot-10 center who would become the greatest shot-blocker in Shocker history. All earned first-team all-conference honors in 1961.

THE ARTIST Miller got a tip on Gene Wiley through Linwood Sexton, WU's All-America halfback in the mid-1940s. Sexton had a relative in Amarillo, Texas, and that's how WU first heard of this raw-but-gifted center.

But there was a problem. Wiley had twice dropped out of school and had a full year of courses to go before he could graduate high school. So Miller arranged to have Wiley move to Wichita, get a part-time job to pay expenses and get his diploma from East High. He also took some art classes, helping what would become his post-basketball career.

Wiley played no basketball at East, but it was a small sacrifice for the Shockers. Once at WU, he quickly established himself as one of the nation's premier blocked-

From Wichita North, Joe Stevens was a dependable guard who twice led the Shockers in scoring.

Lanny Van Eman led WU over powerful Cincinnati in 1961.

shot artists. His 80 blocks in 1961-62 is easily a school record, and the top six blocked-shot games in Shocker history all belong to big No. 12.

Of the Shockers' 10 triple-double games in 89 years of basketball, Wiley owns four of them. Every time, he had double digits in points, rebounds and blocked shots. After WU, Wiley played four seasons with the Los Angeles Lakers and another two years in the ABA.

TEXAS PIPELINE FLOWS AGAIN While the Shockers were having a good season, Miller's staff was working hard on bringing in two more huge pieces to the puzzle.

A friend of Miller's, who worked in Fort Worth, got into a conversation with Olympic sprinter Stonewall Johnson on a flight to Dallas after the 1960 Rome Olympics. When the subject turned to basketball, Johnson said he knew of the best player in Texas.

His name was Dave Stallworth.

Quickly, the scouting reports came back. Miller's friend said he was the best prep player he had ever seen. Miller's brother and assistant, Dick, came back from Dallas and sung his praises.

Somehow, no other major schools were after Stallworth, who was a mid-semester graduate. He would be a Shocker.

But Dick Miller scored again on the same trip to Dallas. Playing against Stallworth that night was a 6-10 center who was a little raw but obviously promising.

Given the opportunity to play college ball with Stallworth, Nate Bowman headed north to Wichita, as well.

IT ALL COMES TOGETHER

Over the years, Shocker basketball has always been regarded as the talk of the town. For two periods, though, Wichita was crazier about the Shockers than at any other time. From 1960-65 and 1980-85, the city followed its team with a fervor and enthusiasm that made the Roundhouse shake and kept its glorified players going in big game after big game.

In the early '60s, though, it was a new feeling. Teams of the late '50s had struggled, and a couple years of success weren't enough to fill the Roundhouse. Attendance in 1960-61, when WU was 18-8, averaged only a half-full 5,333.

But if Ralph built it, they would come.

BEARCAT BATTLES In the '50s and '60s, there was no greater rival to come to the Roundhouse than the University of Cincinnati. Year after year, the Bearcats would bring a top-notch, highly ranked team in to face the Shockers, with or without Oscar Robertson.

Shocker center Gene Wiley twice earned All-Missouri Valley honors.

THE ONE AND ONLY

The banquet room was crowded that March night in 1964. The Shockers finished one victory away from their first Final Four, and fans flocked to the WU post-season celebration to congratulate their boys one more time.

It was a moment Ralph Miller couldn't resist. He strode to the podium and said, "Where were you people when those guys egged my house back in 1959?"

Pure, unmistakable Ralph Miller.

Shocker fans often didn't know whether to love him or hate him in his 13 years as Wichita's head coach. He won, but not enough. He was a good coach, but not an effervescent guy who made boosters happy.

An incident in January 1960 was an example. With less than a minute to go, WU trailed Bradley 71-70 at the Roundhouse but had the ball. In the huddle, Miller gave explicit instructions to wind the clock down to 15 seconds, then get the ball to Lanny Van Eman and let him create a play.

Ralph Miller is the eighth-winningiest coach in college basketball history.

The ball went to sophomore reserve John Allen, who held the ball under one arm. He held it with 15 seconds to go, and still as the final seconds ticked down. Finally, he threw the ball in the air, thinking the Shockers had won. But they had lost.

Some fans were irate. As the team ate its post-game meal, Miller was hung in effigy on campus. Also, fans threw eggs at the Miller home on Stadium, a short walk from the Roundhouse.

"We rode out the tough times," Miller wrote in his 1990 book, "Spanning the Game." "You learn to develop a thick skin in this business. Although people might not have realized it then, better days were ahead."

On Dec. 18, 1961, though, Wichita had an answer. Behind 49-46 with 56 seconds to play, Lanny Van Eman led the charge as WU beat No. 2 Cincy 52-51. Van Eman had 19 points and fans stormed the court after the final gun.

Though the loss broke its 27-game winning streak, Cincinnati won the NCAA title later that season.

RIP 'EM UP, TEAR 'EM UP WU got off to a terrific start in 1961-62, winning 9 of its first 10 and moving as high as No. 8 in the polls. That included a win at No. 6 Purdue and the home win over Cincinnati a week later.

But that would be the high point of the season. Wiley broke an ankle midway through the schedule and was lost for the year, and Van Eman's eligibility was gone by the end of the first semester.

Miller had already decided to insert Stallworth onto

WU was one of very few schools recruiting Dave Stallworth.

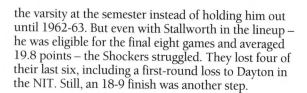

A 19-8 record in 1962-63 was highlighted by wins over NCAA champ Loyola and runner-up Cincinnati.

the varsity at the semester instead of holding him out until 1962-63. But even with Stallworth in the lineup – he was eligible for the final eight games and averaged 19.8 points – the Shockers struggled. They lost four of their last six, including a first-round loss to Dayton in the NIT. Still, an 18-9 finish was another step.

'NONE OF US LET UP' Perhaps the Shockers' finest victory ever came on Feb. 16, 1963, in the Roundhouse. Though ranked, Wichita was still an underdog against No. 1 Cincinnati, the two-time defending NCAA champion which had won 37 consecutive games. That included a 63-50 win over the Shockers a month earlier in Cincinnati.

It didn't look good for WU on this night, either, when Cincy pulled ahead by six with 3:10 to play. But then Stallworth stepped up his game, as if that were possible. Scoring the last seven points, he gave the Shockers the lead for good in a 65-64 victory.

By Dave Stallworth's junior season, WU Fieldhouse attendance increased by 3,000 per game.

Fans flooded the court and carried Stallworth off on their shoulders. In what was the greatest single-game performance by a Shocker, Stallworth hit 14 of 22 shots, 18 of 23 at the free-throw line and ended with a school-record 46 points. He also had nine rebounds.

What the fans didn't know at the time, though, was that Stallworth had an upset stomach during the game. He vomited at halftime and had to sit out the first two minutes of the second half while recovering.

"None of us let up for a second," Stallworth said after the game. "If we had, we wouldn't have won."

STANDING GUARD Miller was faced with an unusual problem at guard throughout the 1963-64 season. Leonard Kelley, a double-figure scorer his entire career, was eligible only for the first semester because he was graduating. Ernie Moore, a sharp defender who was also a double-figure scorer, was eligible for only the final eight games because of an eligibility technicality.

So even though they had been backcourt mates for two seasons, Kelley and Moore never played a game together in 1963-64. Still, they produced. Moore averaged 17.4 points, Kelley 11.1.

What made it even tougher for the Shockers was that sophomore Kelly Pete was forced to fill the other guard spot and learn on the go. It was a problem for about a minute. Pete, a 6-1 All-Stater from Wichita East, was already known as a rebounder, averaging 16 boards on the freshman squad. On the varsity, though, Pete sparkled by averaging 8.8 points and shooting 48 percent from the field.

Kelly Pete stepped in quickly and produced.

SOLID GROUND WU started the season ranked fifth, but a 2-2 start dropped it out of the Top 10. That didn't dissuade the Shockers, who went on a stretch of 15 wins in 16 tries, the only loss coming at Ohio State.

More importantly, Wichita was 7-0 against ranked teams before a loss at No. 17 Drake late in the Valley schedule. That turned out to be a big defeat, because it prevented the Shockers from taking sole possession of the Missouri Valley title. Still, as co-champion, it was WU's first Valley title and the first conference crown for WU since 1932-33.

MORE RAVES Again, Stallworth was outstanding. He scored 30 points in a game 12 times and set six single-season records: field goals and attempts, shooting percentage, free-throw attempts, points and scoring average (26.5).

His most impressive night that season was against – who else – Cincinnati. Down three with 29 seconds to play, Stallworth scored four straight points, made a steal and assisted on another basket as WU won 62-59.

No game was ever over with The Rave on your side.

THE BULLDOG BATTLE When the Shockers beat North Texas State in the regular-season finale in Wichita, Miller was thrown in the shower for a reason: By winning its final four Valley games, WU had forced a playoff with Drake for the Valley's entry in the NCAA Tournament. The neutral site chosen was Kansas' Allen Fieldhouse in Lawrence.

Neutral? Not quite. Of the 14,500 seats in the arena, Wichita sold tickets for more than 10,000 of them. Fans streamed from Wichita to Lawrence by car, bus (28 charter buses was the final count) and even a charter train, which cost a reasonable $8.

Because there were no reserved seats, fans waited outside the gates to get in two hours before tipoff. Once in, Wichita fans weren't disappointed. The Shockers beat Drake 58-50 for their first-ever NCAA berth. Stallworth, who days before had been named All-America, scored 21 points, and Moore, in his final game, scored 21.

And it just so happened that the Midwest Regional was at the Roundhouse.

Dave Stallworth scored a WSU-best 24.2 points a game in his three-year career.

'WICHITA: CAGE TOWN GONE MAD' That was the headline from the March 6, 1964, Wichita Eagle. It was above a story detailing how Shocker fans had become rabid over their most successful team ever. Among the notations:

Ernie Moore drives to the basket against Drake in 1964.

"Instead of a prayer, a prominent minister opens his Sunday serivce with the remark, 'How about that game last night?' ... A television station interrupts a network broadcast to announce that an out-of-town game will be televised."

ONE STEP AWAY The Midwest Regional started the right way for WU. Stallworth scored 18 of his 22 points in the second half and had 23 rebounds as the Shockers whipped Creighton 84-68 in the semifinal.

One night later, it was WU against Tex Winter's Kansas State bunch. For one reason or another, the Shockers and Wildcats hadn't met in basketball since early in the 1950-51 season, a year before Miller arrived at WU. So Shocker fans craved not only a shot at the Final Four but a chance to beat an in-state rival.

The Shockers never really got off the ground in their bid for the Final Four. Behind Murrell and 7-foot center Roger Suttner, K-State jumped to a 13-point halftime lead and never let Wichita get close. The final was 94-86.

Wichita's best basketball season ended at 23-6, with its first Valley championship and second All-American. And a big, bright future.

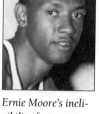

Ernie Moore's ineligibility for postseason was a key in WU's 1964 Midwest Regional troubles.

NEXT STOP, IOWA CITY Days after the 1964 season, Miller's name came up with numerous coaching vacancies. At Kansas, Miller was for a short time a candidate to take over for Dick Harp. But because WU was entering the state's higher education system (and becoming Wichita State),

KU could not hire him. Instead, Ted Owens got the job.

But Miller and his wife, Jean, agreed to visit Iowa. They liked it, and in March 1964 the Hawkeyes had a new coach. In 13 seasons at WU, Miller was 220-133.

Any Shocker fan knows Miller's route from there: six years at Iowa, 19 at Oregon State, eighth on the collegiate career victories list and a spot in the Naismith Hall of Fame.

"There was a little Joe Namath quality (in him), which means you're cocky if you say something but you're confident if you produce what you say," Van Eman told The Wichita Eagle in 1985. "Ralph was a great producer. As a result, he was a controversial person. When he left Wichita in 1964, I don't think everyone would have joined in unison and said there was a great loss. I think people realized after he left what a great person he was."

Ralph's last words to Wichita: "Thanks for 16 years of thrilling and wonderful memories."

TO THE FINAL FOUR

It seemed only natural that Gary Thompson, former player and Miller disciple, take over when Miller left for Iowa. Thompson had been a top assistant for seven seasons and bled black and gold. And with the pieces in place for another great season, why mess things up with a new regime?

Thompson had plenty of credentials. He played six years for Miller at Wichita East and WU, and was a starting guard on the 1954 NIT ballclub. Add to that his record as the freshmen team coach: 60 wins, 12 losses.

But could the Shockers get past the loss of their old coach and take that next step, to the Final Four in Portland? It was an amazing road.

Gary Thompson moved up the bench to take over the Shockers.

HIGH EXPECTATIONS Certainly the rest of the country thought Wichita State was a contender for the national title. The Shockers began the season ranked third in the AP poll behind Michigan and UCLA.

Double-digit victories over Long Beach State, Texas Western, and Brigham Young twice didn't hurt, either. When the Shockers took the court in Detroit against Michigan in their fifth game on Dec. 14, 1964, it was as the top-ranked team in the country.

It was WSU's first, and so far only, No. 1 ranking.

A HEAVE AND A PRAYER Cobo Hall in Detroit was rocking for a matchup of the nation's top two teams. Stallworth's star quality was matched by Michigan's Cazzie Russell.

A tight game all the way, it was tied at 85 with seconds remaining. Russell got the ball for the Wolverines and launched a 35-foot shot as the buzzer sounded. It went in, giving Michigan an 87-85 victory and ending

4. What three Shockers were first-team All-Valley in 1965?

The 1964-65 team has been WSU's most successful, winning the '65 Midwest Regional to qualify for the Final Four.

WSU's run at No. 1. The Shockers bounced back with a 71-60 win at Drake five days later, but dropped to No. 2 in the next poll.

'LEACH'S CORNER' The story goes that the first time Miller watched Dave Leach play basketball, Leach was supposedly the third-best player on a strong McPherson High team. Miller was told that two other Bullpups were better, but he held firm and offered Leach a scholarship instead.

Good move. Leach was a key outside shooter for the Shockers when teams focused their defensive efforts on Stallworth and Bowman. He became such a dead-eye, fans started referring to the left corner of the court as "Leach's Corner." Leach, who was later an assistant to Miller for 10 years at Oregon State, averaged 12.3 points as a senior.

NO, NO, NATE Wichita State was 12-2 overall and 5-0 in the Valley after an 11-point win over St. Louis is mid-December. But then the Shockers began to unravel.

Five days later, Thompson dismissed center Nate Bowman after he was declared academically ineligible for the second semester. Bowman was averaging 12.4 points after earning second-team all-conference honors the previous season. It was a big blow to WSU because it meant that Leach, at only 6-5, would be the center. Once Stallworth's eligibility expired two games later, no Shocker would be taller than Leach or sophomore Melvin Reed.

By beating Drake in the final game, WSU won consecutive MVC crowns for the only time.

THE MUNCHKIN BUNCH Without Stallworth and Bowman, the look of the '65 Shockers changed dramatically. Yes, rebounding was no longer an asset, but they were able to make some adjustments to make up for a lack of height. For example, Leach guarded the opposing team's center, but on offense would remain outside as WSU's top shooter. In a man-to-man, that meant the opposing center was on Leach and away from the basket.

A pleasant surprise was the play of Jamie Thompson, a 6-3 sophomore who took Stallworth's place. In his first

DAVE'S LAST RAVE

It was another sellout in the Fieldhouse, another big Missouri Valley Conference game for a Wichita State team having a tremendous 12-3 start.

But oh, every fan knew what this game on Jan. 30, 1965, was all about. It wasn't Louisville vs. Wichita State. It was Dave's final game.

Even Ralph Miller took some time away from his first season at Iowa to come back for Stallworth's final appearance in an emotional Roundhouse, the place where The

Dave Stallworth spent 10 seasons in the NBA, seven with the New York Knicks.

Rave solidified WSU's role in the college basketball world.

And as if there were any question, Stallworth dominated again. A night after scoring 45 points in an overtime loss at Loyola (Chicago), Stallworth scored 40 points as WSU won easily 96-76.

Stallworth left the game after completing a three-point play with 35 seconds to go. He received a thunderous ovation, then after the game was lauded by university president Emory Lindquist, Miller, Gary Thompson and teammate Dave Leach.

When his career numbers were tallied, Stallworth owned 18 Shocker records and two years of All-America honors. Heck, The Associated Press named him to their second team in 1964-65 even though he played in only 16 of WSU's 30 games.

Thirty years later, Stallworth still holds five WSU marks, and his three-year statistics (1,936 points, 24.2 average) are easily the most impressive in Shocker history. Given a fourth year, as WSU's other top six scorers were, The Rave would have rewritten the record book.

After Stallworth received gift after gift from WSU supporters, he was given the microphone for some final words. He simply said, "It's been my pleasure playing for you."

No, Dave, the pleasure was ours.

game as a starter – and WSU's first without The Rave – Thompson scored 21 points as the Shockers won at St. Louis 72-64.

Thompson turned out to be one of WSU's finest players, scoring 1,359 points and twice earning All-Valley honors. He hit a school-record 85.3 percent of his free throws and in 1966-67 was named to the national All-Academic first team.

MIDWEST IN MANHATTAN By winning the MVC, the 19-7 Shockers earned another berth in the Midwest Regional, this time at Ahearn Fieldhouse in Manhattan. The opponent was Southern Methodist, the 16-9 Southwest Conference champs whose five starters were all averaging double figures.

There was no favorite among the Midwest Regional entrants. One Wichita Eagle sportswriter noted that many thought the Shockers were living on "borrowed time," what with the midseason departures of Stallworth and Bowman.

But the Shockers weren't fazed by anything in Manhattan. Pete scored 31 points and had 12 rebounds as WSU beat SMU 86-81, setting up the regional final a night later against Hank Iba's Oklahoma State team.

FOR PETE'S SAKE Exhausted from a tight, 40-minute game just 24 hours earlier, the Shockers had little time to rest before meeting Oklahoma State.

HAIL WICHITA! WSU fans go for the net after the Shockers beat Oklahoma State in the 1965 Midwest Regional final at Ahearn Fieldhouse in Manhattan.

Once the tipoff came, there was no more rest. Gary Thompson played five players – Pete, Leach, John Criss, Vernon Smith and Jamie Thompson – the entire way. With half the fans from Wichita, the Shockers rode the momentum in a low-scoring game, winning 54-46.

Pete was magnificent, scoring 19 points with nine rebounds despite having a 101-degree fever. The game was also sweet for Smith, who played his first season at Stillwater for the Cowboys. He beat his old teammates, and in the process kept Iba from taking the career victories lead from Kentucky's Adolph Rupp.

Next stop, the Final Four.

"I don't think we can win at Portland," Gary Thompson admitted, "but the boys think we can and they may make me believe it."

The 1965 Final Four featured three future NBA stars: Bill Bradley, Cazzie Russell and Gail Goodrich.

BRUINS BREWIN' The underdog label fit Wichita State throughout the 108-89 loss to UCLA in the national semifinals. The defending-champion Bruins were bigger, stronger, faster and jumped better than WSU, which got 36 points from Jamie Thompson.

UCLA, which would eventually beat Michigan for the title, jumped ahead of the Shockers with a mid-first half run that had WSU down 65-38 at the half. Gail Goodrich had 28 for UCLA.

THE KING OF PRINCETON The next night Wichita State would unwillingly take its place in Final Four history.

Kelly Pete takes a shot for WSU against Princeton in the third-place game at the 1965 Final Four in Portland.

Warren Armstrong, left, and Kelly Pete were two of four double-figure scorers on the 1965-66 team.

From the 1961-62 through 1965-66 seasons, WSU was 61-4 at home.

5. Name the two tallest players in Shocker history.

That was when the Shockers gave up 58 points to Bill Bradley, Princeton's Rhodes Scholar who turned in a record-setting performance in the Tigers' 118-82 walloping of WSU for third place.

"We had no special plans for this game," Gary Thompson said. "We had hoped Bradley would get his usual 25 or 30 and we could stop someone else."

Didn't happen. Bradley made 22 of 29 shots, 14 of 15 foul shots and got 17 rebounds. Given instructions to shoot at every opportunity in the final 3 1/2 minutes, Bradley broke Oscar Robertson's seven-year-old Final Four record of 56 with 38 seconds to play.

LONG TRIP HOME Wichita State's first, and so far only, Final Four could not have gone much worse. WSU gave up 226 points and was blown out early in both games.

"I offer no apologies for being here," Gary Thompson said. "We earned the right, winning the Missouri Valley and our regional. Our showing here is a very, very bitter pill for the boys to swallow.

"We had two miracles and we were hoping for a third."

KEEPING UP THE MOMENTUM

The rest of Thompson's days as coach of the Shockers were uneventful. The Shockers won four high-scoring games to start the 1965-66 season and slipped into the polls at No. 10, but it didn't last long and WSU wouldn't see the national rankings again for 15 years.

But the late '60s had its share of Shocker stars.

REVENGE One of Thompson's biggest wins came in the second game of the 1965-66 season. Hosting No. 2 Michigan, the team that knocked off WSU while it was No. 1 the previous season, Wichita State won 100-94 at the Fieldhouse.

The Shockers were slower and not as strong at ballhandling as Michigan, "but the greatest bunch of basketball scrappers in this land banished all my concerns," Thompson said after the game. In his second varsity game, sophomore sensation Warren Armstrong was held scoreless by Russell in the first half, but had 16 in the second. Jamie Thompson had 28 points, missing only one shot.

PETE'S PROWESS Thompson pulled no punches when describing Kelly Pete's contribution to the Shocker program.

"Kelly is the best guard in the history of Wichita State University and very possibly the standout guard in the nation this season," Thompson said before Pete's senior year, 1965-66.

Pete was the leader of the Shockers the previous year, when WSU withstood the loss of Stallworth and Bowman to win the Midwest Regional and earn its first Final Four berth. Pete was a tremendous defensive player, though he was also a pretty good threat from the outside.

EYES ON THE BALL There may never have been as versatile a Shocker as Warren Armstrong, who played from 1965 to 1968. First, consider that the three-time All-Valley performer averaged almost 17 points for his career, then consider that as a sophomore, he set two school records that didn't have anything to do with scoring.

He set a Shocker record with almost 12 rebounds a game in his first season, and he also set a single-game record with a dozen assists. Like Gene Wiley, he owns four of WSU's 10 triple-double games (points, rebounds, assists, or blocks in Wiley's case).

Armstrong, who was 6-2 and later played in the ABA for seven seasons, was successful not only because of his superior vertical leap and peripheral vision, but also because he was an unselfish player who'd give up a shot for a teammate's easier chance.

WSU toured South America during the summer of 1966, playing outdoors once in 33-degree weather.

6. What was Warren Armstrong's nickname?

What's wrong with this picture? Coach Gary Thompson and an injured Warren Armstrong pose for media pictures before the 1966-67 season.

PICKIN' SLIM They called him "Slim" because at 6-foot-5, he weighed only 160 pounds. Yes, Ron Washington was the slimmest Shocker from 1965-69.

But he had a silky-smooth jump shot that was at its best with a high arc. If not for a couple of bouts with a dislocated shoulder, he might have moved higher among the Shockers' career scoring leaders. As it was, Washington scored 1,013 points (14.7 average) and averaged almost seven rebounds.

THE FAT LADY SANG When is a basketball game not 40 minutes long? When the fans say it isn't. On Feb. 1, 1967, Wichita State led Drake 71-60 in Des Moines. With 11 seconds to play, Drake center Bob Netolicky missed a dunk, and that was enough for the unruly Bulldogs fans. Many threw coins onto the court and caused such a delay that the referees decided to give the game an early exit.

THE BACKGROUND LEADER Overshadowed by players such as Warren Armstrong, Greg Carney and Ron Washington, Ron Mendell never led a Shocker team in scoring, but he was a key ingredient in all three Shocker teams he played for. From Ottawa, Kan., Mendell aver-aged 12 points for his career but more importantly was a good defensive guard who was strong in several areas. He became the Shockers' second Academic All-American in the '60s, earning the honor in 1968-69.

Ron Washington was nicknamed "Slim" for obvious reasons.

NO ADJUSTMENT NECESSARY The 1967-68 Shocker media guide speculated that although Greg Carney was a highly touted recruit out of high school in Chicago, he would need time to regain his scoring touch in college because he was academically ineligible for his one season on the freshman squad.

Yeah, right. Carney averaged 15.9 points as a sophomore and became WSU's most prolific scoring guard, averaging 20.1 points for his career. Carney was at his best when driving to the basket, either hitting the short shots or drawing fouls.

Twice, Carney's efforts earned him first-team honors on the Small Man All-America team and he was first-team All-Missouri Valley twice, as well.

Greg Carney was only 5-foot-9, but he averaged 20.1 points in his three seasons.

SAME NAME, NEW FACE Despite the efforts of Armstrong, Washington, Carney, Mendell, Terry Benton and others, Thompson was fired after a fourth straight losing season, the first time that had happened in Shocker Country since 1948-52. WSU athletic director

Harry Miller won an NAIA championship before coming to WSU.

Cecil Coleman decided it was time for a change. Thompson "was not retained primarily on his seven years and what was accomplished in my judgment," Coleman said. "The money spent on the program was not commenserate with the results." Thompson was 93-94 in seven seasons.

The replacement was somewhat surprising. Harry Miller had been coach at Valley-rival North Texas State only a year, compiling a 10-15 record. But he owned an NAIA title at Eastern New Mexico in 1969, and his career winning percentage was a shade under .700. He also knew Coleman when they both worked at Fresno State.

His task? To be as successful as the Shockers' last Miller.

THE BALL IS MINE One player that Miller inherited, he knew all too well. Terry Benton was the same guy who pulled down 29 rebounds in the Shockers' game against Miller's North Texas State bunch the previous season.

Benton, a 6-foot-8 post player from Wichita East, had a nose for the basketball that only the great rebounders have. In his junior season, he grabbed 20 or more rebounds in seven games and averaged 16.8 overall. Both are school records 25 years later.

In a three-game conference stretch that season, Benton hauled in 69 rebounds in three games. That helped him earn All-Valley honors that season and in his senior year, when he averaged 16.2 points and 14.0 boards. Only once his junior season did he pull down fewer than 10 rebounds in a game.

HARRIS-ING START Miller had plenty of personnel to get started, especially a talented and experienced front line of Ron Harris, Vince Smith and Benton. All would be 1,000-point scorers.

Harris, who averaged almost 17 points in his career,

Terry Benton was one of the most prolific rebounders in WSU history.

Despite 18.5 points and eight rebounds per game over his last two seasons, Ron Harris was never an All-Valley pick.

Only 6-foot-4, Rich Morsden was an effective center, averaging 8.6 rebounds over his final two seasons.

Robert Elmore was three-time All-Valley and was among the nation's leading rebounders.

had his biggest night four games into Miller's tenure. WSU beat Southern Illinois 91-83 behind Harris' 46 points, one short of Stallworth's school record. Harris made 16 of 20 shots and 13 of 15 free throws.

VALLEY IN THE VALLEY Miller's first team finished 16-10, but a 1-7 start the next season started a three-year slide where the Shockers went 32-46.

There were still stars. Rich Morsden, the smallest center around at only 6-foot-4, averaged 15 points as a junior and made All-Valley. Vince Smith, though always left off All-Valley teams, averaged double figures for three years as WSU's best outside threat. And Bob Wilson averaged 19 points in two seasons after an All-America career at Northeastern (Colo.) Junior College.

Then there was "Wild" Bill Lang, a rough 6-5 forward from the streets of Chicago. "I've broken my nose seven times and never had it set," Lang once said. "I broke it three times playing basketball, once in hockey and the rest in fights."

MO MAKES AN APPEARANCE He came to Wichita State with only two years of basketball experience, one in high school and one in junior college. But Shocker coaches knew that Robert Elmore and his 6-foot-10, 245-pound body were going to be special.

Coming from Jamaica, N.Y., Elmore was academically ineligible for his sophomore and junior seasons in high school, but picked it up by his senior year. Still a little

green, he opted for the junior-college route. A foot injury two games into WSU's 1973-74 season made him red-shirt for a year, but he came back the next season and immediately became the Valley's dominant big man.

All three of his seasons, he led the Valley in rebounding and was the All-MVC center. Short on finesse but with plenty of muscle and power, there wasn't a player around who could move Big Mo. His 15.8 rebounding average in 1976-77 was third-best in the nation.

Calvin Bruton took his skills from the playgrounds of New York to the floor of Levitt Arena.

RETURN OF THE WINNING WAYS Miller's best Shocker team was in 1975-76, when the makings of a Valley champion were there. Elmore had molded into the conference's best big man; Calvin Bruton was a senior and as good a one-on-one player as there was in the Midwest; and a promising freshman named Lynbert Johnson enrolled at WSU from New York.

Throw in solid players such as Robert Gray, Bob Trogele and Neil Strom, and Wichita State had its best team in 10 years. The Shockers finished 18-10 and conference champs for the first time in 11 seasons.

CHEESE, PLEASE Lynbert "Cheese" Johnson came to the Shockers as one of the school's most highly publicized high school players. From New York's Haaren High, he was on everybody's All-America or Top 10 lists of recruits.

But with the help of first-year assistant Ed Murphy, WSU landed Johnson and reaped the benefits for four seasons. His game was no secret even early his freshman season, when he led the Shockers in scoring his first three collegiate games, all easy wins against lesser opponents.

The story goes that Johnson got his nickname because his first name sounded similar to Limburger, a type of cheese. That, plus Johnson's constant smile, earned him the most recognizable nickname in Shocker basketball history.

"Cheese can do anything he wants to on the basketball court," Miller said. He was right. Johnson averaged 11 points and seven rebounds as a freshman, shooting 58 percent and earning MVC Newcomer of the Year honors.

7. What other sport did Calvin Bruton excel at?

CHAMPS AGAIN The 1976 Valley race was no pushover for the Shockers. West Texas State was ranked much of the season, and Southern Illinois was a threat with sharp-shooter Mike Glenn.

But Wichita State, without leading the conference in any significant statistical categories, won all the important games. The Shockers lost to both West Texas and SIU on the road, but won 10 of 11 games down the stretch to win the Valley by a game over the Salukis.

Elmore led the Valley in rebounding for a second straight year, earning all-conference honors. Bruton and

8. What was guard John Kobar's nick-name?

Gray, a forward who averaged a team-high 13.3 points, were named to the second team.

The next stop was a little rusty for WSU: the NCAAs.

RIVALRY RENEWED WSU and Michigan hadn't met since 1965, when the Shockers knocked off the No. 2 Wolverines 100-94 in Wichita. But here they were again, matched up in the first round of the NCAA Tournament at Denton, Texas.

WSU led by 13 early in the second half, but was caught late. With six seconds to play and the Wolverines down one, Rickey Green hit a jumper from the left side to give Michigan a 74-73 lead. WSU's desperation shot at the buzzer didn't go, ending the Shockers' best season since 1964-65. Despite three early fouls, Elmore led WSU with 18 points.

Robert Elmore and Cheese Johnson were both first-team All-Valley in 1976-77, as WSU again finished 18-10.

Afterward, Michigan coach Johnny Orr called WSU the second-best team his bunch had faced all season – right behind Indiana, the team Michigan would meet and lose to in the national championship game.

THE HIGH SPOTS There were two memorable victories in the 1976-77 season. The first was in Levitt Arena on Feb. 5, 1977, when WSU squeaked by Southern Illinois 91-90 in double overtime. Johnson had 28 points, Elmore had 22 rebounds, but both were overshadowed by SIU's Glenn, who had 40 points.

Eight months after his college career ended, Robert Elmore died of a heroin injection in Rome, where he was playing in an Italian pro league.

The other big win was at Marquette on Feb. 19. The Shockers won 75-64 in what was Al McGuire's final home game as coach of the Warriors. Johnson and Elmore each had 19, with freshman Ray Shirley and sophomore Charlie Brent adding 13 each.

Less than two months later, McGuire retired with the 1977 national championship.

WHEN HARRY MET THE ROAD Statistically, Johnson's junior season was his best yet. He averaged 19 points and 10 rebounds, shooting a career-best 55 percent. But all that was only good enough for second-team All-Valley notice.

Why? Because the Shockers were a mediocre team in 1977-78. They finished 13-14 overall, 8-8 and in fifth place in the MVC, and lost to Bradley in the first round of the Valley tournament. Attendance at Levitt dipped to less than 7,800 per game, and Miller was fired after a 97-90 career record. That's when four simple letters took Wichita by storm.

M T X E

You'd read it on the sides of the players' jerseys, shorts and warmups. You'd read it on the coach's towel. Heck,

Gene Smithson preached MTXE 24 hours a day.

after a while it was painted onto the court itself.

MTXE. Mental Toughness, Xtra Effort. Gene Smithson's creed for his Shocker basketball program. Chosen over 108 other applicants and after a 66-18 record in three years at Illinois State, Smithson wanted nothing less than full throttle.

"MTXE is something which I have styled my life after, going full speed and giving everything which I can give to reach my self-imposed goals," Smithson said in his first season, 1978-79.

Under Gene Smithson, WSU scored more than 90 points every night of a six-game winning streak. Up tempo was back.

As a basketball plan, it meant the Shockers would play an up-tempo, high-pressure defensive style that Wichita hoops fans seem to clamor for. As a personal motto, it meant Smithson was always on the go.

"No one can ever say I wore out a suit sitting down at courtside," he once joked.

The Smithson Era at Wichita State was some of the most exciting basketball played in the Roundhouse. He won two-thirds of his games, including back-to-back-to-back 20-win seasons, the first time that had been done in Shocker Country. He also brought in some of the best players, who took WSU twice to the NCAAs, twice to the NIT and only once below third place in the Missouri Valley.

MTXE was never boring.

9. *Who was the first recruit inked by Gene Smithson?*

BIRD'S BOYS One game that Johnson didn't lead the Shockers in, though, was the one in which Larry Bird and undefeated Indiana State invaded Levitt Arena. Johnson missed the game with a sprained ankle suffered in the previous game at Drake. It deprived the crowd of 10,584 of a matchup of All-America candidates.

Cheese Johnson's injury prevented a matchup with Larry Bird.

No. 5 Indiana State, which wouldn't lose until the 1979 national championship game against Michigan State, won 94-84 even though Bird sat the final seven minutes of the first half with three fouls. WSU hung tough, getting a career-high 27 points from forward Ray Shirley.

Was Cheese worth 10 points? Too bad we'll never know.

LUV YA, CHEESE Wichita State finished an even .500 all around in Smithson's first season, overall (14-14) and in the conference (8-8). Not a bad year, but a season that will certainly be remembered as Johnson's last.

Playing 35 minutes a night, Johnson averaged 22.2 points, at that time the fifth-best mark in Shocker history, and left as the school's second-leading rebounder. He was also the first Shocker to shoot better than 50 percent all four years (Antoine Carr and Xavier McDaniel later matched that).

Cheese went out in style on Feb. 17, 1979, in his final

Cheese Johnson had a terrific senior season, averaging 22.2 points and 10.6 rebounds.

Gene Smithson's 1979 recruiting class was probably the school's best incoming crop of talent ever. From left: Ozell Jones (standing), Mike Jones, Antoine Carr, Chris Boyd, Auguster Jackson, James Gibbs, Jay Jackson, Randy Smithson and Cliff Levingston.

home game. Early arrivals among a standing-room-only crowd of 10,731 received cardboard cutouts of Johnson on a stick, with the words at the bottom, "SMILE AND SAY CHEESE."

With his mom and dad in the crowd, Johnson played all 40 minutes and responded with 27 points and 13 rebounds as the Shockers nipped New Mexico State 86-84.

HAPPY DAYS ARE HERE AGAIN

The next four years returned to the glory days of Shocker basketball. It was easier to dig for oil with a shovel than dig up an extra ticket for a home game. The Shockers won 91 games and lost just 28 in that stretch, winning the conference twice and finishing second the other two times. And 15 years after WSU's only Final Four appearance, the town was living and dying by every Shocker game.

Eagle reporter Jon Roe summed up a fan's feeling in 1981: "When you buy a season ticket, you move into a neighborhood. You chat with your neighbors about families, jobs, plans, hopes, dreams. And, of course, the team. You didn't know most of these people before and perhaps wouldn't want to. But, inside the arena, they are

Behind freshmen Cliff Levingston and Antoine Carr, WSU made the NIT field with a 16-10 record.

part of the party."

Yes, Wichita State basketball entered the early 1980s as a big party. A party where everybody always seemed to go home happy.

RESPECT COMES SLOWLY With almost everybody back, plus junior-college point guard Tony Martin and Wichita West product Karl Papke, Wichita State had a stellar start in 1980-81. WSU started with seven wins, lost 2 of 3 over the holidays even though it had big leads in both, then won another 10 straight.

BARNUM AND BAILEY BREDEHOFT

Ted Bredehoft stood before a group of media and well-wishers that day in 1972 and made a statement that would stand for his 10 years as Wichita State's athletic director: "There are 82,246 square miles in Kansas and I'd like to declare all of this country as Shocker Country."

Oh, how he tried. From Camel Races to Shocker Bread to booking Evil Knievel and the Dallas Cowboys Cheerleaders, oh how Ted tried.

He was an energetic, 5-foot-4, 40-year-old assistant AD from Arizona State when WSU brought him to the Midwest. The headline above the story of his departure in the Phoenix newspaper said, "Wichita, Are You Ready for Ted Bredehoft?"

Were we? Well, it took some getting used to. Among the Bredehoft innovations, crazy schemes or whatever you want to call them:

■ There was the Shocker Mountain Ski School, the 5,400-square-foot artificial ski slope under the west stands of Cessna Stadium. It made money for a while.

■ Or the 16 different organizations fans could belong to, highlighted by the Black Gold Club (minimum crude oil donation of $150), the Golden Bushel (minimum donation of $50 in bushels of wheat) and the Beef Club (a simple side of beef would do).

■ Or a money-back guarantee for football season-ticket holders when the Shockers lost a home game.

To Bredehoft's credit, he was a strong fund-raiser who developed athletics from a five-sport program to 15. He was the man who hired Gene Stephenson to revive a base-ball program, he was in charge

Still, the Shockers were snubbed in the national rankings, and that caused some hard feelings. ". . . There's no doubt in my mind we should be ranked," Randy Smithson said. "I know we're better than KU. If they're 18th, we're fifth. They're a joke for a ranked team."

The rankings finally came. The Shockers entered at 19th and climbed as high as 14th before a loss at Indiana State knocked them out.

MORE ON THE WAY Even before the Shockers started the '80-81 season, good news had already arrived. Greg

when WSU beat Kansas in basketball and football in a 1 1/2-year span, and he was an innovator with his idea of the Shocker Sports Channel, a pay-cable product that televised all home basketball games when they were long sold out.

What soured Bredehoft's tenure, though, were three NCAA investigations that resulted in three probations. The last one, in football, probably led to his forced resignation late in 1982. Also in

Bredehoft's decade at the helm, 23 athletic department workers were fired or forced out in the first two years, and 50 workers came and went, including nine sports information directors.

But to many fans, Bredehoft was a master showman and just the right man for WSU. Those folks undoubtedly still have their Shocker clickers and bread wrappers to prove it.

Whether it was after a big win, hawking Shocker souvenirs or promoting a ski school on the plains, Ted Bredehoft did everything with flair.

GOOD NEWS AND A.C.

Cliff Levingston came from the sunshine of San Diego, Antoine Carr from the heart of the Midwest. But the one thing they had in common – excelling at basketball – made them bond as friends in just a couple of days.

Levingston was All-State in California his final high school season, while Carr was on everybody's All-America list. Carr had long since signed to attend Wichita State when he met Levingston at the Dapper Dan Roundball Classic in Pittsburgh after the 1978-79 high school season.

Instantly, Carr and Levingston became friends, and Carr did a little recruiting by convincing Levingston to join him at WSU, choosing the Shockers over Marquette, Minnesota, UCLA and several West Coast schools.

"Cliff and I are a pair," Carr later said. "We like being called a pair. We're not worried about any limelight."

Oh, but they got plenty of limelight as a pair. Levingston was the workhorse, averaging more than 10 rebounds all three seasons and dominating inside the lane. Carr, an inch taller at 6-9, could go outside more with a better shot, but he also was great at driving inside for a soft shot or thunderous dunk.

The two forwards quickly got the nickname "The Bookends." In their final two seasons together (Levingston turned pro after his junior year), the Shockers won 49 games, a school record, and lost just 13.

"It's real important that me and Antoine like each other," Levingston once said. "Because we can't play against each other. It would hurt the team if we tried to outdo each other. Instead, we work together."

Dreiling, a 7-foot-1 center being recruited by every college with two hoops and a ball, announced in November 1980 that he would stay home after his days at Kapaun Mount Carmel and attend WSU.

Wichita's other All-American, Heights' Aubrey Sherrod, waited until the spring to decide on the Shockers. That meant that of the five City League All-Americans in a six-year span (Carr, Sherrod, Dreiling, Darnell Valentine and Ricky Ross), the Shockers landed three.

THE NCAA COMES KNOCKING The opening paragraph stirred up Wichita much like an annoying alarm clock on that Monday morning, Feb. 2, 1981.

"The Wichita State University Shockers, an emerging basketball powerhouse, are one of the best teams money can buy," wrote the Kansas City Times for everyone to see.

Word quickly got to Wichita about the Times' story, a first in a series about cheating in Midwest universities. By far, though, Wichita State was hammered harder than any other.

After a three-month investigation, the Times reported some WSU basketball players under Smithson accepted cash, clothes, airline tickets and loans that were never repaid from coaches and boosters. The NCAA was already investigating, and its findings wouldn't be known for a year. But the effects of the stories were almost immediate.

Prep All-Americans Greg Dreiling, above, and Aubrey Sherrod, below, would join forces at WSU.

OZELL'S ODYSSEY As if anything else could go wrong off the court, Ozell Jones was declared ineligible for the Valley tournament because of a technicality with his high school transcript.

In high school at Long Beach, Calif., Jones' grade-point average was calculated including his physical education classes. His clammates' GPAs did not include P.E. That's an NCAA rules violation, even though 90 percent of the high schools around the country compute P.E. classes into overall GPAs. And because Jones' GPA was not above the minimum 2.0 without the P.E. classes, he was declared ineligible.

But not before Jones got a temporary restraining order. Jogging into Levitt Arena for the Valley first-round game against Southern Illinois, he got a loud ovation and scored 12 points with seven rebounds.

But the restraining order wouldn't stand. Jones played in the second-round victory and championship-game loss to Creighton, but was not allowed to go any further into the NCAA Tournament. Jones later played at Cal State-Fullerton, and WSU fans never got an idea of how good a center he could be.

"You just don't lose a guy who's been part of your team all season and not feel it," Randy Smithson said.

Ozell Jones took a backseat to "The Bookends" but was an effective center.

WELCOME HOME The MVC loss and Jones' courtroom loss had the Shockers' limping into the NCAAs. After losing to Creighton, it wasn't even known if WSU would get to stay home for the first two rounds.

But the NCAA granted that wish, putting WSU against Southern University and Kansas against Mississippi in the Midwest Regional's first round at Levitt. Iowa and Arizona State received first-round byes.

Wearing black shoulder patches in honor of Jones, the Shockers decimated Southern's fast-break game with outside shooting and rebounding, winning 95-70. KU defeated Ole Miss 69-66 to the delight of Shocker fans, who had a WSU-KU matchup in the backs of their minds.

TIME OUT, TIME OUT Levitt Arena has seen a number of magical moments, but maybe never one so unbelievable as the 1981 Midwest Regional second-round game between Wichita State and Iowa. It was the day 10,666 emotions built into one continuous roar, seemingly lifting their Wichita State team to greater heights.

As with all great comebacks, though, there was a slow start. Iowa led 36-25 at halftime, then scored the first

Cliff Levingston, center, tries a shot against Iowa in the 1981 Midwest Regional at Levitt Arena.

four points of the second half.

The Shockers were on the ropes. But the crowd kept pushing them back into the middle of the ring.

Down 15 with 18:53 to play, WSU went on the greatest rally in school history: Fifteen unanswered points over a span of 8 minutes, 50 seconds. Carr scored six in the stretch, Cliff Levingston five and Randy Smithson four.

But tied at 40, the Shockers could never get over that hump. Possession after possession, with a rabid crowd pleading for two points that would surely sink the Hawkeyes, they never came.

Until the end. Tied at 56 after Smithson fed Carr for a layup, Iowa called its final time-out with 17 seconds to play, setting up a last shot. But Kevin Boyle missed and Carr was fouled as he got the rebound with five seconds to play.

That's when Iowa coach Lute Olson signaled to reserve Bobby Hansen for a time-out. Only the Hawkeyes had already used their five. It set off a frenzy that's probably still reverberating through Levitt's rafters. Carr missed his one-and-one, but Smithson hit both technical shots ("It sent shivers through me," he said) and Carr hit two after a foul on the inbounds play. Final score, 60-56.

"It was a mixup in communications between me and Hansen," said Olson, who slapped himself in the head after realizing his mistake.

"The turning point in the game was the crowd," Jay Jackson said. "It affected us, and it affected them."

Maybe Eagle-Beacon columnist Steve Love put it best: "When talent fuses with emotion and the people off the floor become a part of what is happening on the floor, almost anything is possible."

SHOCKS AND HAWKS Those WSU fans who still had heartbeats hung around the arena that Sunday afternoon to see Kansas surprise third-ranked Arizona State 88-71, setting up a KU-WSU Midwest Regional semifinal in the Louisiana Superdome.

Was there ever a crazier week in Wichita?

ANOTHER HUMP As if anything else could cause a setback to this Shocker team, Martin suffered back spasms in the latter part of the Iowa game and was listed as doubtful for the Kansas game. Originally called a ruptured disc, he was close to surgery when the diagnosis was switched to an inflamed disc. Either way, Martin was done.

"We're still a fine team," Smithson said. "Moreover, we're a team that has great character. We'll reach down a little bit further and find a little bit more in ourselves."

And a little bit more in Martin. He recovered quickly, leaving the hospital a day before the game and joining the team flight. He took shooting drills and participated

10. Who gave Cliff Levingston his "Good News" nickname?

Always looking for an edge, Ted Bredehoft placed an ad in the New Orleans and Baton Rouge papers, asking LSU fans to root for WSU over Kansas.

in the rest of practice.

On a team full of stars, Martin was an integral part at point guard. Always pushing the ball upcourt, He was a great ballhandler who allowed Randy Smithson to play his natural off-guard spot.

The Shockers' itinerary for game day against KU:
3 p.m. – Pregame meal
5 p.m. – Leave for Superdome
5:30 p.m. – Arrive at Superdome
7:08 p.m. – BEAT KU
1 a.m. – Bed check

ON THE BATTLEFIELD The outcome of the Battle of New Orleans seemed pretty simple, really: Could WSU's guards handle Darnell Valentine and Tony Guy of KU? Or could KU's big men (Art Housey, John Crawford, the really big Victor Mitchell) shut down WSU's bookends?

Mostly, it was a draw. Wichita State led much of the first half but needed a Mitchell technical for hanging on the rim (Smithson made a free throw) for a 33-32 halftime lead.

But the momentum changed a bit in the second half when KU went on an 8-0 run to take a 42-41 lead with 14:27 to play. The Jayhawks would trail for only 14 seconds the rest of the way – until the end, of course.

Antoine Carr plays interior defense against Kansas' John Crawford in the Battle of New Orleans.

MASSACRING VALENTINE'S DAY The end of the first KU-WSU game in 36 years was great if you were a Wichita State fan, but maybe sad if you were a fan of Wichita basketball.

KU had the game in hand with 56 seconds to go, leading by three and with a reliable Valentine at the line for a one-and-one. Valentine was the greatest point guard in

THE SHOT HEARD 'ROUND THE STATE

Mike Jones had been sitting on the bench for almost five minutes when Gene Smithson sent him back into the game with 1:15 to go.

With WSU trailing Kansas 65-62 and the Jayhawks packing it in on bookends Cliff Levingston and Antoine Carr, the Shockers were going to have to win or lose from the outside.

And with Jones, those were usually your choices. Seconds after a great shot, he'd clank one off the backboard. Following a sly steal, he might throw a crosscourt pass into the band.

But Smithson had little choice but to go with a streaky shooter such as Jones. His first bomb came with 47 seconds to go and got WSU within one. Then, after KU's Darnell Valentine missed an easy layup, the Shockers had one more shot.

KU crunched the zone in on Carr and Levingston, so Randy Smithson, Tony Martin and Jones passed around the perimeter, looking for the best shot. In the corner, the more reliable Smithson didn't have it. So with five seconds to go, Jones began the most famous shot in Shocker history.

"Mike Jones isn't scared to shoot them," Gene Smithson later said. "He's not shy – especially if he gets a few to go down."

This one did, giving WSU the 66-65 victory. Always a bit player in the Shocker scheme of things,

Jones was for once the toast of the town. Both shots are listed as 25 feet on the stat sheet, but you'd have a hard time convincing anyone who was there they were that close.

"Sometimes I get frustrated and try to do things all at once," Jones said. "But I took my shots at the right time tonight."

Mike Jones lets fly with the biggest shot in Shocker history.

Wichita City League history, heading the state's best-ever high school team at Wichita Heights to the 1977 state championship. Always a class act, he was a terrific ambassador and example of the quality of Wichita basketball.

But he missed the free throw. Then, after Mike Jones' bomb cut the lead to one, Valentine got a perfect baseball pass from Guy for a layup. But he missed that, too.

Levingston got the rebound, WSU called time-out, Jones hit the game-winner with two seconds left, and Valentine's career was over.

"I just missed the layup," he would say later. "I should have made it. In these kinds of situations, you can't be passive."

BRING ON LSU Black-and-gold fans partied hard on Bourbon Street that Friday night in New Orleans, but everywhere they went, they were outnumbered by LSU fans. The fourth-ranked Tigers had blitzed Arkansas in the late semifinal, setting up a Sunday showdown that

Antoine Carr and Gene Smithson embrace after WSU's 66-65 thriller over Kansas in the Louisiana Superdome.

wouldn't see LSU fans cheering for WSU.

A favorite LSU chant became, "What do we eat? Shocker meat!" No WSU follower took the time to explain that there's no meat on a shock of wheat.

Didn't seem to matter. Playing against a talented front line and against 35,000 screaming Cajuns, WSU lost to the Tigers 96-85 in a bid for its second Final Four, ending the season 26-7 and advancing further than any Shocker team in 16 years.

"These guys have nothing to be ashamed of," said Randy Smithson, a senior. "I'm sad because it is my last moment. But I'm leaving knowing that we have put Wichita State on the map.

"We've brought it back from the dead, and it is here to stay."

TESTING YOUR FAITH No Shocker basketball tickets were more coveted in 1981-82 than student seats. So coveted, in fact, that 30 students were ready to miss a test just to keep their places in a long line.

Minutes before the test was scheduled, one of the students ran into a teaching assistant who would be administering it. Informing the assistant of how many students would miss the test, it was postponed and 200 other students who had their No. 2 pencils ready were sent home.

"It wasn't just inconvenience, it said something about priorities at this university," one student said. "What gets me is that I wanted basketball tickets, too, but I thought I had a test to take and it came first, so I didn't get in line. I ended up no test, no tickets."

GUNNING FOR NO. 1 The 1981-82 Shocker team had arguably more talent than any other. Carr and Levingston were destined for pro careers, Martin led the show, and Aubrey Sherrod, Greg Dreiling and Xavier McDaniel formed a freshman class rivaling the one two years earlier (and don't forget Mike Jones, whom Shocker fans could never rightfully disparage again).

WSU started the season ranked sixth and won its first seven games before Christmas, including a 75-60 domination of No. 9 Alabama-Birmingham in Levitt Arena.

As the Shockers headed for the Rainbow Classic two days after Christmas, the were ranked third and soon headed for No. 2.

MAINLAND, AND STEP ON IT Despite three ranked teams in the eight-school Rainbow Classic in Honolulu, WSU was the talk of the island as it took over the No. 2 ranking the day it defeated Cal State-Fullerton 70-67.

But the talk soon turned to what was wrong with the Shockers. North Carolina State, ranked 20th, outscored

Because of packed houses, WSU created the Shocker Sports Superchannel, a pay-cable service that televised home games.

11. Who won the 1981 Rainbow Classic?

WSU 24-6 at the foul line and won 60-48. It was the fewest points scored by a Smithson team in a loss.

It wasn't much prettier the next night. No. 6 San Francisco beat the Shockers 84-74, giving WSU fourth place.

"It would be nice to come back and visit, but to come back and play again," Martin said, "that would be something else."

WSU got revenge over LSU in 1981-82 with a 66-65 victory at Baton Rouge.

OTHER SHOE DROPS Finally, almost a year after the Kansas City Times' series, the NCAA made its report public. Wichita State was handed three years' probation, including two years of sanctions that included no postseason play. Carr and Levingston would not play in the NCAAs again.

Though some Times allegations weren't substantiated by the NCAA, plenty were. They included airline tickets and other transportation for players, cash, clothing, breaking of tryout and recruiting rules, meals, lodging and unethical conduct by two former assistant coaches. The charges were based on events from 1975 to 1980, roughly even between the Harry Miller and Smithson regimes.

WHOLESALE CHANGES Assured of no postseason play until March 1984, the end of the 1981-82 season brought more questions than answers.

Would the Bookends go to the NBA? Half would. Cliff Levingston applied for the NBA draft and was taken as the ninth pick by the Detroit Pistons.

Then Greg Dreiling announced he was leaving WSU after his freshman season to attend Kansas. He said the NCAA sanctions had little effect, but "I think I kind of need to get away from Wichita and my hometown. My experience at WSU as a basketball player wasn't a bad one."

Antoine Carr stayed home, though. "Because of my love for my teammates and the community, it's my desire to be remembered as one of the former greats of Wichita State. I'm going to forgo financial security and conclude the Antoine Carr era at Wichita State," he said.

"Antoine says he wasn't indispensible," Smithson said. "But I beg to differ. A.C. was the catalyst to this program when he signed with us and now, down the line, he becomes the catalyst again.

"He's the one who really solidifies our basketball team."

A stress fracture was the only thing stopping Antoine Carr at WSU.

MORE THAN ONE LEG TO STAND ON Perhaps the best thing to happen to the 1982-83 Shockers was Carr suffering a stress fracture in his leg. Without him, the young Shockers had to grow up in a hurry.

What a hurry. With Xavier McDaniel roaming the middle with much more authority than his freshman season, the Shockers upset the powerful Soviet National team 81-80 in an exhibition game.

Without Carr in the lineup, WSU won five of its first six games. Once Carr returned, the Shockers were 20-2 and finished their finest season ever.

COME AND GET US How powerful were the '83 Shockers? Consider that the Valley's leading scorer was Carr, more than three points ahead of the pack at 22.6 a game. The leading rebounder was McDaniel, who at 14.4 led the nation.

Whether it was shooting percentage, scoring, rebounding or most other statistics, the Shockers dominated the Valley. The 17-1 conference mark, blotted only by a 54-53 loss at Illinois State, was a mere formality.

YOUR STAT CREW OR MINE? As McDaniel's rebounding prowess became more widely known, he also had his detractors. One was Bradley coach Dick Versace, who commented that McDaniel was being helped by a "homer" stat crew that was inflating his totals.

So in the Shockers' next-to-last game of the '82-83 season, McDaniel made it a personal mission to make Versace eat his words. Playing on Bradley's home floor with the Braves' stat crew, McDaniel was a one-man terror. He scored 34 points, snared 20 rebounds, hit 11 of 16 shots and 12 of 15 free throws as WSU won 97-96 in double overtime.

Dick Versace was made a believer of the X-Man.

"He's a brilliant basketball player," Versace later said. "He has the greatest work ethic I've ever seen."

'WITH A BANG' The day before Carr's last game, he made no secret about his desire to end with something special. "Hopefully, I'll go out with a big game and leave everyone with good memories," he said.

And how. Carr put on the best offensive display ever seen at Levitt Arena, scoring 47 points to eclipse Dave Stallworth's record by a point. Hitting 21 of 36 shots and 4 of 6 free throws, Carr was a scoring machine that didn't shut down until he got the record with a shot from the right baseline in the final seconds.

(Fans of asterisks will note that one of Carr's field goals was a three-pointer, which wasn't around in Stallworth's day and was used only experimentally in the 1982-83 season.)

When it was over and a sold-out Roundhouse thundered its approval for Carr, he broke down just before raising his retired jersey above his head. "If you ever had a feeling you didn't want to leave some place," he said, "that's the feeling I had. I really don't want to leave because people have been so kind to me."

Antoine Carr dunked his way to All-America status in 1983.

Yugoslav center Zarko Durisic was a fan favorite.

WHERE'S THAT STRIPE? How many more points would Aubrey Sherrod have scored had the three-point line been in existence during his playing days? Consider that WSU's career three-point leader, Paul Guffrovich, sank 144 in his four years. Then realize that Sherrod regularly shot from that range with no line, and certainly would have attempted more out there with a line.

Surely, Sherrod's sweet flick of the wrist would be worth another 150-or-so points, putting him within reach of the McDaniels and Littletons of the Shocker scoring world. As it was, he was the perfect foil when defenses were packing it in around McDaniel, Carr, Levingston or whoever else was dominating inside. Sherrod ended his career as WSU's leading backcourt scorer with 1,765 points.

JAMMIN' IN JAPAN WSU went to the Suntory Ball in Japan trying to find itself early in the 1984-85 season. But with No. 10 North Carolina the first opponent, there wasn't much time for investigation.

The Shockers played the Tar Heels even for much of the game, but a lull and the end of the first half and beginning of the second was the difference. Outscored 14-3 in that stretch, WSU lost 80-69.

McDaniel had 23 points and nine rebounds, battling inside with 6-11 Brad Daugherty and 6-10 Joe Wolf. Amazingly, it would be the only time in his senior season McDaniel would not have double figures in points and rebounds.

The Shockers were in better shape a day later against Arizona State in Tokyo. They led most of the way, but McDaniel twisted his knee and missed the end of the game after scoring 30 points and grabbing 11 rebounds. With him out, WSU scored just three points in the final seven minutes and lost 66-65.

WSU and Kansas renewed its basketball series after 31 years in 1984, with the Shockers losing 79-69 at Lawrence.

With a flick of the wrist, Aubrey Sherrod was an outside weapon.

12. In only four seasons in Shocker history have there been four future 1,000-point scorers on the floor at the same time. Name the four seasons.

X'S BEST Even with a sub-.500 non-conference record, which dipped to 4-7 after a 90-83 loss to Kansas at Kemper Arena, the Shockers still had high hopes in the Missouri Valley. A 98-64 win over West Texas State was a good start.

In Game 2, at Bradley, McDaniel had his finest day as a Shocker. Hitting 16 of 24 shots and 11 of 18 free throws, he scored a career-high 43 points and grabbed 20 rebounds as WSU won 82-79. It was nothing new for McDaniel against Bradley, though. Later in the season, he had 33 points and 22 rebounds.

As McDaniel was pulled near the end of that game, Versace walked to him and shook his hand. "I told him he's a fantastic ballplayer and he's had a hell of a career," Versace said. "We've seen so much of him, he seems like he's one of our family."

ANOTHER HURRICANE WARNING Finally, the schedule-makers got one right. Wichita State and Tulsa met on the final day of the Valley regular season, with the conference championship on the line. Both teams, as well as Illinois State, were 11-4 heading into the game at Tulsa.

WSU owned a 13-point lead with 15 minutes to play, but no lead is safe in this series. Tulsa fought back and went ahead 67-65 with 21 seconds to play. The Shockers worked for a final shot and point guard Mike Arline was fouled with three seconds to go.

Arline made the first foul shot but missed the second.

Somehow he got his own rebound, and his desperation shot agonizingly bounced off as the buzzer sounded. With Illinois State choking, Tulsa was the regular-season champ.

But there would be another showdown in T-Town.

A BETTER ENDING Exactly a week later, after first- and second-round victories, WSU again caught the bus to Tulsa for the Valley championship game. This time, the lead was big again but there wasn't much time for the Hurricane to come back. Surely, a 15-point Shocker lead with 4:44 to go was safe.

But this was WSU-TU. Tulsa's Steve Harris scored 24 of his 37 points in the second half as the Hurricane pulled to within two with eight seconds to go.

WSU had the ball, but lost it. "I was trying to get the ball to Papke," Sherrod said. "He got it knocked out of his hands and I grabbed it. Then, I got it knocked out of my hands. The next thing I know, Harris is shooting."

It was one of those off-balance, buzzer-beating attempts that seem to go in and turn the home crowd into a rabid frenzy. But this one didn't fall and WSU had won 84-82 for an NCAA berth after a 3-6 start.

THE FORGOTTEN ONE A main hero from the Valley victory was Papke, a 6-6 swingman from Wichita West who had experienced ups and downs as a Shocker. The only remaining member of the last NCAA Tournament team (1981), Papke redshirted the 1981-82 season with a shoulder injury. He had worked his way back slowly and was rewarded with a big game against Tulsa: 12 points, nine rebounds, seven assists and a good open-court game against Tulsa's press.

DOGGIN' IT WSU's first NCAA bid in four years wasn't a pushover. The Shockers drew 19th-ranked Georgia in the East Regional and in the Bulldogs' own back yard: the Omni in Atlanta.

McDaniel was phenomenal in a first-half deadlock, scoring 18 of WSU's 27 points. But Georgia readjusted its defense after intermission, putting two and three players around him and constantly changing looks. McDaniel took only six shots, made two and finished with 22 points.

Meanwhile, Georgia went on a 12-0 run aided by seven Shocker turnovers. By the time the rally had ended, WSU was down 47-33 and it got only as close as seven the rest of the way, losing 67-59.

"That one stretch was where we let the game get away," Smithson said.

END OF AN ERA Shocker fortunes fell quickly the next season. With 4 of 6 top players gone, including the indispensible McDaniel, a group with no seniors struggled through the middle of the season, losing eight straight in one stretch to finish the season 14-14.

That was the end for Smithson. Athletic Director Lew Perkins announced Smithson's dismissal two days after the Shockers' Valley tournament loss, citing declining

X'S SPOT: AMONG THE GREATS

The story goes that Xavier McDaniel, a freshman from South Carolina with only a couple of months on the Kansas plains, sidled up to juniors Cliff Levingston and Antoine Carr, the two guys who lifted WSU to within one game of the Final Four.

McDaniel looked his elders in the eyes that first day of basketball practice and said, "One of you is going to have to sit down."

Well, it took a season for McDaniel to draw comparisons to other Shocker greats, but the ferociousness and intensity in which

Xavier McDaniel's senior season was one of the NCAA's all-time best.

McDaniel played was evident from Day 1.

At 6-foot-8, 205 pounds, he played the game as few players have. Every shot was under control, as his 56.4 shooting percentage attests. Every rebound was his, no matter where it bounced.

"I just hope one day before I quit coaching basketball that I get one like him to coach," Creighton's Willis Reed said.

McDaniel was no better than in 1984-85, the season in which he became the first Division I player to lead the nation in scoring and rebounding in the same season.

He averaged 27.2 points to 26.3 for Loyola's Alfredrick Hughes. He outrebounded Creighton's Benoit Benjamin 14.8 to 14.4 during the season, and 34-26 during their two head-to-head meetings. Benjamin was four inches taller, of course.

McDaniel scored 30 points 13 times in his final season and had four 20-rebound games. He was named first-team All-America by both the Associated Press and U.S. Basketball Writers Association and became only the third Valley player to score 2,000 points and grab 1,000 rebounds.

But mainly, X was The Man.

"It was an honor for me to have coached the player who was first in history to accomplish this," Smithson said. "It's unbelievable. But he's unbelievable."

attendance, community apathy and a poor academic record among Smithson's players.

Smithson came and left with 14-14 seasons, but in between came the best run in Shocker history. His teams averaged 19.4 wins a season, and he was the only coach to guide WSU to back-to-back 20-win seasons, which he actually did three straight years.

THE CAROLINA WAY

Eddie Fogler's pedigree certainly was top-notch: assistant to possibly the top high school coach in the country (DeMatha's Morgan Wooten), assistant to possibly the top college coach in the country.

But in March 1986, Fogler was ready to go out on his own. "I just left one of the best jobs in the country," Fogler told the media on his arrival as WSU's new basketball coach. "I wouldn't leave one of the best jobs in the country to come somewhere that wasn't a good opportunity."

Fogler spent 19 years at North Carolina, four as a player and 15 as an assistant to Dean Smith. There he learned the Carolina system that he would employ at Wichita State.

"I think we have found one of the most outstanding young coaches in the game today," Perkins said. "He's been trained by the best."

He would soon have the Shockers in the spotlight again.

Even with WSU's long basketball tradition, Eddie Fogler was only the second coach to lead consecutive 20-game winners.

TAKE THAT, SISTERS In his first try, Fogler accomplished what no other Shocker coach had done: beat intrastate rivals Kansas and Kansas State in the same season. First, Dwight Praylow made a driving layup for a three-point play with two seconds to go, giving WSU a 63-60 victory over K-State.

Six games later, No. 19 Kansas played in Levitt Arena for the first time since Phog Allen helped old student Ralph Miller dedicate the Roundhouse 31 years earlier. This time, the Shockers won 54-49 in a game dominated by a slow-down style that Fogler designed. All-American Danny Manning had just 12 points and didn't score in the last 11 minutes, 55 seconds.

One of Eddie Fogler's first moves was to get rid of black road uniforms and go to yellow.

CONFORMING INTO WINNERS There were plenty of interesting stories in Fogler's first season – such as 6-9 Yugoslav Sasha Radunovich, whose style of play was often too flamboyant for Fogler. Radunovich's ball fakes, in which he'd hide the ball between his knees and fake a quick pass, often got him a seat on the bench.

Or there was Henry Carr, who was often called Hank, which rhymed with Clank, as in free-throw shooting.

Sasha Radunovich was an imaginative basketball player.

The younger brother of Antoine Carr, Henry had bettered 50 percent foul shooting only in his freshman year, and by his junior season was shooting a horrid 36 percent. But working with assistant coach Mike Cohen, Carr came up with a routine that was odd, to say the least.

At the line, Carr would extend his arm underhand toward the basket, appearing to hand the ball down the lane. He would bring it back to shooting position and let fly with a high, arching shot. Sixty percent won't get you in the NCAA leaders, but for Carr, it was a miracle.

STRANGE GAME NO. 1 Fordham and WSU met in the 1986 Shocker Shootout, Fogler's fourth game at the helm. WSU blew a 15-point lead and went into overtime, then another.

Fordham was ahead by eight with less than 10 seconds

to play when the most bizarre ending occurred. Shocker Gary Cundiff hit a three-pointer with one second to go and called time-out trailing 91-86. Thinking the game was over, a Fordham player dumped a water cooler on Coach Bob Quinn. Water spilled onto the court and Fordham was assessed a two-shot technical foul.

Cundiff made both, then WSU got the ball at half-court needing a three-pointer with one second to play. Gus Santos got the ball, turned and fired in a 30-footer for the apparent tie, but officials ruled the shot came late and the most amazing comeback in Shocker history was thwarted.

It was the only game WSU lost at Levitt in Fogler's first year.

PASSING THE TESTS By the close of Fogler's first regular season, WSU was 19-10 and third in the Valley, already an amazing season. But things were just getting started.

There was the first round of the conference tournament, when Creighton owned a 19-point first-half lead in Wichita, only to see the Shockers come back to win 73-70. Or there was the semifinal at Levitt, when Illinois State led by 15 with 14 1/2 minutes to play. But WSU held ISU to only five points the rest of the way, winning 56-53.

All that set up another WSU-Tulsa conference tourney final, again in Tulsa. Unlike the first two tourney games, WSU played extremely well, only to have Tulsa catch up by the end. But the Shockers took control in overtime and won 79-74 for the NCAA automatic bid. Cundiff, a guard who had once been given up on by the previous coaching staff, responded in true senior fashion with 17 points on 6-of-7 shooting.

Henry Carr shot free throws for everyone to see.

Henry Carr, Eddie Fogler and Gary Cundiff celebrate after the Shockers won the 1987 Valley tournament with an overtime win at Tulsa.

BUZZER-BEATING BALDI WSU's first-round opponent in the Midwest Regional was St. John's, which wasn't so bad considering the Redmen weren't too quick and agile for the Shockers. It was an even game throughout, and the score was tied at 55 when St. John's guard Mark Jackson was trapped at half-court with six seconds to play.

But Jackson found seldom-used center Marco Baldi, who had gotten away from Radunovich for an off-balance, 15-footer at the buzzer. It went in.

Marco Baldi?

The Eagle-Beacon's Fred Mann portrayed it well: "Marco Baldi is a 6-foot-11, 245-pound guy from Aosta, Italy, who plays basketball sort of like the Leaning Tower of Pisa would if it had legs. He is slow, but he generally makes up for it with a lack of shooting ability. He averaged all of 3.8 points per game for the St. John's Redmen this year, coming off the bench to spell the world-renown Terry Bross at center."

DUPED BY DePAUL With much the same team in 1987-88, Wichita State had a few lows (three consecutive overtime losses in December) but mostly highs. The Shockers ran over No. 18 Bradley 116-92 in Levitt Arena, though the Braves would win the conference crown.

A 20-win season assured with a first-round tournament win over Tulsa – WSU's third win over TU in 16 days – the Shockers found themselves in the Midwest Regional at South Bend, Ind., facing DePaul.

It was the first blowout WSU suffered all season. DePaul led 16-6 just 6 1/2 minutes in and was never threatened. Led by standout guard Rod Strickland, DePaul forced 21 Shocker turnovers and won 83-62. Still, WSU had back-to-back 20-win seasons for the first time in five years.

STRANGE GAME NO. 2 It was a sight that drove Shocker fans nuts as they were tuned to their TVs on Feb. 23, 1989. There were their five guys in gold, trying to figure out how to score against an Indiana State team with only four players on the floor.

After a fight in which Indiana State's Darin Lyles attacked Radunovich, WSU's John Cooper was ejected for throwing a punch, and all ISU reserves were tossed for leaving their bench, WSU had a 5-on-4 advantage for the final 22 minutes.

Leading by 15 immediately after the fight, WSU won by 15. Indiana State's four (Jeff Lauritzen, Jimmie Holliday, Townsend Harris and Ron Cheatham) played the rest of the way, spurred on by a rabid Hulman Center crowd. At one point, the Sycamores were within four.

"It was just different, we didn't know what to do," WSU's Dwight Praylow said. "For playing 4 on 5, they played pretty well. It was just a weird, weird game."

MOVING ON A third straight NCAA trip wasn't in store for the Shockers. WSU finished 19-11 after a second-round NIT loss at Michigan State. Nine days later, Fogler announced he was leaving for Vanderbilt after winning 61 and losing 32 at WSU.

"I can honestly say it's one of the toughest, if not the toughest, decisions that I've made in quite some time," Fogler said. "A lot tougher than deciding to leave North Carolina to come to Wichita State three years ago."

At his final Wichita news conference, Fogler recommended that his top assistant, Cohen, replace him as head coach. One week later, Cohen was the man.

'I'M READY FOR THE CHALLENGE' If Eddie Fogler was the strict tactician around Levitt Arena, then Mike Cohen was the kind, father figure.

"I think all the players were happy with the decision," guard Keith Bonds said. "He is very emotional and very

The WSU All-Number Team

00 Ozell Jones
3 Paul Scheer
4 Gary Thompson
10 Preston Carrington
11 Calvin Bruton
12 Gene Wiley
13 Cleo Littleton
14 Bob Hodgson
15 Paul Guffrovich
20 Steve Grayer
21 Jim McNerney
22 Greg Carney
23 Bob Trogele
24 Ron Mendell
25 Ray Shirley
30 Kelly Pete
31 Cheese Johnson
32 Jamie Thompson
33 Rich Morsden
34 Xavier McDaniel
35 Antoine Carr
40 Lanny Van Eman
41 Doug Yoder
42 Dave Stallworth
43 Rex McMurray
44 Ron Washington
45 Sasha Radunovich
50 Terry Benton
51 Charles Brent
52 Warren Armstrong
53 Robert Elmore
54 Cliff Levingston
55 Neil Strom

Mike Cohen was emotional at the news conference announcing his hiring.

excited about this job."

Emotional? That was evident from the day he took the job. Breaking down often during the news conference, Cohen said fans "might see an awfully emotional team that I'm coaching next year."

The losses of Gaylon Nickerson (transfer) and Aaron Davis (heart problem) hurt WSU's depth in 1990-91.

It was the first time as a collegiate head coach for Cohen, who had been in coaching for 25 years. Shocker AD Tom Shupe said: "He's a blue-collar kind of guy who has come up through the ranks. There was no silver spoon in his career. What he got, he earned."

But what Cohen got were a ton of losses and some bad luck that not many coaches could overcome.

BIG INJURY, BIG WIN Almost lost in the craziness of Dec. 3, 1990, at Levitt Arena was the Shockers' first win over a ranked team in almost two years. WSU topped 12th-ranked Alabama 74-71 in overtime, the biggest win in Cohen's career, but the game will be remembered just as much for Cohen himself.

WSU took a 33-31 lead on Claudius Johnson's basket at halftime, and as the Shockers hustled to the tunnel, Cohen was bumped from behind and fell to the floor, rupturing the patella tendon in his left knee.

Mike Cohen makes his point.

Cohen's knee was examined, but he came back in the arena two minutes into the second half wearing sweat pants, a WSU sweater and resting on crutches. "I'm glad it's me going into surgery tomorrow and not any of the kids."

Two games later, with Cohen using his crutches as pointers toward officials, Wichita State upset Oklahoma State 72-69. "I felt better on my wedding day," Cohen said, "but next to that, this is the happiest I've ever been."

HAWAII FIVE-OUCH The fun and sun of Honolulu quickly turned bleak for the Shockers early in the 1990-91 season. Against Tennessee in the first round of the Rainbow

John Cooper was the steadiest of Shockers until an injury his final season.

Classic, John Cooper drove to the basket late in the game and was tripped by the Volunteers' Steve Rivers. Cooper broke his left ankle, falling to the ground in pain.

WSU won the game 77-73, but there were only tears in the locker room afterward. "The games just don't seem to mean as much right now," teammate Tony Johnson said. "It's a tragedy to have him gone."

Cooper had already played in more than 20 percent of WSU's games, so he wasn't eligible for a redshirt season. His stellar Shocker career, which included 1,153 points, was over. With a full senior season, Cooper would probably have moved among the Shocker top 10 scorers.

"You never think it's going to happen to you," Cooper said. "But the timing of this really stinks."

CHANGING TIMES WSU continued a downward trend, losing 16 of 18 under Cohen at one point in his third season. With 10 games remaining in the regular season, he announced his resignation, effective at the end of the schedule. Cohen's last Shocker team finished 8-20, the worst WSU record since 1950.

THOMPSON TAKES OVER

Eleven days after the season, Scott Thompson walked into Levitt Arena late on a Monday night and met his new challenge. It was a place Thompson was well familiar with.

In 1981, Thompson sat on the bench with Iowa's Lute Olson as a Hawkeye assistant. He had played at Iowa and was an All-Big Ten performer in 1976, but his memory of Levitt was the way the crowd lifted WSU to victory over Iowa in the Midwest Regional. He looked around the arena and told the fans and media, "I know what this place can do to people."

Thompson, 38, was regarded as one of the bright, young head coaches in the game. After 10 years as an assistant at Notre Dame, Iowa and Arizona, he had taken an undistinguished Rice program and in five years built a 20-game winner.

"We'll build here for the long term," Thompson said. "I've never taken a job that I thought was a stepping stone."

AIR ARNOLD Jamie Arnold quickly established himself as Thompson's talented freshman, becoming WSU's third freshman in 49 years to lead the team in scoring, rebounding and shooting percentage (Cleo Littleton and Cliff Levingston were the others).

With only one varsity high school season under his belt, Arnold averaged 11.7 points and nine rebounds and

Scott Thompson wants to bring the thunder back to Levitt Arena.

was the first freshman to earn team MVP honors since Levingston did it 14 years earlier.

GETTING THE POINT Although Thompson's first three years weren't winning ones (a 32-49 record), he did get the most out of a couple of transfer guards.

In 1992-93, Jimmy Bolden transferred to WSU from St. Mary's College in Michigan for his senior season and averaged a team-best 13.4 points. Then two years later, with a season-ending injury to point guard Keith Stricklenl, Thompson had to rely on L.D. Swanson, a 6-2 senior, to take the point.

L.D. Swanson was Mr. Clutch during the 1994-95 season.

Swanson, who played more forward as a junior in his first season from Jacksonville (Texas) College, changed his game from surprising rebounder to surprising point guard. He also was responsible for some exciting Levitt Arena finishes.

Three times in 1994-95, Swanson made game-winning shots in the final seconds or at the buzzer. Averaging 14 points, he hardly ever came out of a game and led WSU to a 13-14 record, the Shockers' best finish in six years.

Baseball

It sat on the south side of 21st Street, between a couple of parking lots: a big patch of grass that wasn't used for anything except for short-iron practice by golfers preparing for a round at the nearby Wichita State course.

But it was there that Gene Stephenson saw his dream. Green grass would remain in some places, but artificial turf, grandstands, locker rooms, concession stands and a press box would be built.

QUIZ

13. The 1949 College World Series was played in Wichita. Who won it?

As the Shockers dominated on the diamond, Stephenson would build around it. He often collided with Athletic Director Ted Bredehoft about the growth of the facility, yet still developed teams that could win games whether there were 15,000 fans in the stands or 15 sitting on bleachers atop flat-bed railroad cars.

WSU's baseball evolution on 21st Street has been a never-ending process. Even now, with one of the finest collegiate facilities around, there is hope for more.

Sure, there was Shocker baseball before Gene Stephenson, but nowhere near the success, recognition and pride.

And there was no national championship.

The 1906 Fairmount team shut out rival Friends 20-0, which would stand as the school's biggest shutout victory for 76 years.

BEFORE THERE WAS GENE

Oh, the university knew all about baseball before Stephenson. In fact, baseball is the second-oldest sport at WSU behind football. It was April 14, 1899, when the Fairmount College debate team was to travel to Winfield for a meet with Southwestern College. Sometime before

that, it was decided that the two schools should engage in a doubleheader: baseball first, then debate.

Fairmount lost the ballgame but won the debate. The Sunflower account:

Whoop! Whoop! Whoop! Victory!

"In future years, some precocious Fairmount student, reveling among the musty archives of our college, will read: 'On the 14th day of April, A.D. 1899, in the Village of Winfield, occurred a wordy discussion between the College of this Village and the College of Fairmount, located in the city of Wichita. Which aforenamed discussion resulted in a –

Ki yi yi! Sis Boom Bah!
Fairmount! Fairmount!
Wich-i-ta!

"The two great events of the 14th were the base ball game and the debate. The first was a victory for the other fellow, the latter a glorious conquest for

Brek-ke-kek kex! Coax! coax!
Brek-ke-kek kex! Coax! coax!
Whoo up! Whoo up! Parabeleu!
Fairmount!

There is little detail about Fairmount's first ballgame. But baseball evolving from debate, huh? Considering umpire-head coach discussions, it seems only fitting.

14. *What pitcher started for WSU in the second game of the 1966 opening day doubleheader?*

THE FIRST PROFESSIONALS Fairmount baseball teams enjoyed mixed success over the years, but a couple of players found their way to the major leagues. Claude Hendrix, a pitcher for the 1908 team, twice led the National League in winning percentage and played eight years with the Pirates and Cubs. Lloyd Bishop, a pitcher and first baseman at Fairmount, played five seasons with the Indians.

MR. VERSATILITY A 1952 Sunflower columnist noted that WU's slick-fielding shortstop, Dick Sanders, always felt jinxed if he had his picture taken before a ballgame.

Photographers and spectators usually waited until Sanders was on the field, anyway. A three-sport star at WU, Sanders was at his best in baseball. He had a great glove and hit in the heart of the Shocker order for three seasons.

Sanders, from Wichita North High, also was a two-year starting quarterback on the football team and played

Dick Sanders mugs for the camera – apparently after a game.

guard on Ralph Miller's first WU basketball team. But after his junior season, he signed a pro contract with the New York Yankees. He just missed making the major leagues but had eight years in the minors.

Sanders was also a force in Wichita's National Baseball Congress national tournament. He's a member of the Shocker Hall of Fame, the NBC Hall of Fame and the Kansas Baseball Hall of Fame.

Don Lock played eight years in the big leagues.

LOCK THE KEY He played for only one winning baseball team, but outfielder Don Lock would make his mark on the sport after WU. Coming from Kingman, Lock twice earned All-Missouri Valley Conference honors. He also played basketball for three years under Miller.

Originally signed by the Yankees, Lock played eight major-league seasons with Washington, Philadelphia and Boston. He was also a minor-league manager for two years.

YER OUT Despite some winning teams in the 1960s (including a divisional conference crown in 1966), baseball was in trouble. There had been three previous stretches before 1970 when there was no baseball at WSU, so the news on May 16, 1970, came as little shock: The program had been eliminated. The reasons given were the lack of a facility and funding.

But throughout the '70s, there were rumblings of baseball's return. Athletic Director Ted Bredehoft wanted to increase the number of programs, and baseball was among the top of the list. Enter a man with a vision.

HE'D SOONER WIN

Gene Stephenson, sans mustache, came to WSU with big dreams.

What kind of person would take on the challenge of starting up a baseball program that had lain dormant for eight years? After all, there was no stadium, no players, and not much interest among Shocker fans.

But Gene Stephenson, a fresh-faced 31-year-old assistant coach from the University of Oklahoma, didn't appear to be a guy who avoided challenges. When he met the media as WSU's baseball coach on Feb. 11, 1977, he pulled no punches.

"We want to win," he said. "I've never been associated with anything less than winners."

That was true. OU had been a fixture at the College World Series in Stephenson's six years as an assistant. And as chief recruiter, Stephenson said he knew of 200 top players.

The baseball budget was only $40,000, which included coaching salaries and scholarships. But Stephenson knew what it would take to build a winner.

"I need seven or eight in key positions and surround

them with walk-ons, average players," he said. "I need three pitchers who can win, a catcher, two infielders and an outstanding outfielder.

"I believe we can surprise a lot of people. A lot of people will want to schedule us, figuring it will be an easy victory."

Opponents would soon learn that Stephenson and the Shockers were serious about making their mark on the college baseball landscape. As if his words that February day weren't enough of a warning.

"I'm planning on a four-year program," Stephenson said. "In the fourth year, hopefully we will be in a position to challenge for the College World Series, hopefully sooner."

As usual, Stephenson backed up his words.

GETTING STARTED Stephenson made it clear what it would take to make WSU a winner: "players plus facilities." So as WSU worked on the facilities, Stephenson went out and got the talent.

There were plenty of good players to be had in 1978, Stephenson's first season. Third baseman Bob Bomerito, one of the great names in Shocker history, transferred from Florissant Valley Community College in St. Louis and hit .431 his first year, finishing second in the nation in doubles (29) and earning All-Valley honors. Right fielder Matt Yeager came from Seward County juco and would hit .385 in two seasons, earning MVP honors both years.

Throw in two more All-Valley players, pitcher-DH Larry Groves and pitcher Rob Burgess, and Wichita State had a good start.

15. What other Shocker sport was eliminated along with baseball in 1970?

16. Who was Gene Stephenson's first high school recruit?

Bob Bomerito had a power stroke to match his name.

The 1978 Shockers made an NCAA-record 147 errors, or almost two per game.

0-1-1 WSU's baseball revival didn't start with a bang. Facing Emporia State in a doubleheader in Fort Worth, Shocker starter Dave Waddell walked five of the first seven batters he faced and allowed two first-inning runs. The Shockers had two solo homers, but three more walks in the third inning accounted for another run and ESU won 4-2.

The day could have been a complete bust, but the Shockers made a three-run comeback in the seventh inning of the second game and tied it at 4 when the game was called because of darkness.

Stephenson wasn't too disappointed in Day 1. "I was pretty happy with our showing considering this was our first real chance to see any type of action out of doors this spring," he said. "Believe me, we'll get much better."

QUIZ

17. Who hit the first home run for Gene Stephenson's Shockers?

HOME AWAY FROM HOME Not until their 18th game of the 1978 season did the Shockers play at home, and even then it wasn't the team's real home field. With Shocker Field still under construction, the city of Wichita leased McAdams Park to WSU for $15 per day game and $35 per night game.

WSU was 20-8 at McAdams before moving into Shocker Field on May 2, 1978. That isn't bad considering the Shockers had exactly zero outdoor practices in Wichita before the home opener. "It's like playing 65 straight road games," Stephenson said.

In 1978, the baseball offices were located in the football film room in the bowels of Cessna Stadium.

NO HITS, NO FANS The 1978 game in which Groves pitched a no-hitter won't be remembered as a pitching masterpiece – it went only five innings because the game ended with an 11-0 run-rule win for WSU over Kansas Newman – but instead for the conditions at McAdams Park that day. The temperature was 50, with a 40 mph wind gusting from the northwest. The 6-foot freshman from Overland Park pitched his no-hitter in front of exactly 24 fans.

HOME IS WHERE THE TURF IS Finally, Shocker Field was ready for its tenants with six games remaining in the regular season. With much to be desired outside the lines, at least there was a top-notch field with a grass outfield and an artificial-turf infield.

WSU finished 43-30-1 in its first season back, though there wouldn't be an NCAA bid for one of only four times in 18 years.

"This field will definitely help our fielding," Stephenson said. "It was tough at McAdams Park." WSU won its first six games on its field, including a two-game sweep of Oklahoma State. The field also featured a $100,000 scoreboard beyond the left-field fence.

There were some down sides, though. Temporary bleachers and a press box inside a mobile home were just two. Wichita Eagle columnist Randy Brown commented, "It's the most pathetic thing I've ever seen." Also pathetic were the lack of restrooms and dressing rooms for the players.

PLAYING LIKE PROS As a way to drum up more interest in a first-year baseball program, the Shockers scheduled an exhibition with the other big-name team in town, the Triple-A Wichita Aeros. The two clubs would meet before the Aeros' American Association game with Iowa.

Pros against collegians? Sure, it was a rout . . . for the collegians. WSU beat the Aeros 7-2, not allowing the Cubs minor-leaguers a single hit. The game was called after 4 1/2 innings because of a prearranged time limit. Five WSU pitchers threw in the 1-hour, 45-minute game.

SIGN OF THE TIMES The Shockers hit 95 home runs in the 1979 season, compared to only 34 for opponents. Joe Carter, a freshman outfielder, had 19, and Dave Howard and Mike Davis had a dozen each.

With the sluggers slugging and the wind often blowing out to left field, a traffic sign was erected on 21st Street beyond the wall: "Caution – Home Run Zone."

SUN, SUDS, HOME RUN BALLS One of the best features of Shocker Field quickly became known as "Piker's Peek." Fans brought coolers, lawn chairs and blankets to the hill beyond the outfield fence to watch Shocker games.

Even though Bredehoft encouraged fans to sit there, he eventually saw dollar signs and put up snow fences and charged fans to sit on the hill.

PLAYING THROUGH PAIN Lose a top hitter for the season and a top pitcher for part of the season and many teams would fold. Wichita State, though, kept ripping up opponents.

Third baseman Bomerito, who hit .431 in 1978, was lost for the 1979 season with a shoulder injury that forced him to redshirt. Groves, WSU's most dependable starter in its first season, missed the first month of the '79 schedule with arm problems.

Still, WSU kept winning. With more depth and experience, the Shockers got off to a 26-5 start. Davis, taking over at third for Bomerito, hit .364 with 12 homers and earned All-Valley honors.

NO HITS, NO RELAXING At 19 years old, 6 feet and 180 pounds, Don Heinkel was a freshman with promise. But on March 24, 1979, Heinkel was shaky against Illinois. He walked the bases loaded with two outs in the first and second innings, hit batters in the second and third, and ended up walking 11.

When it was over, though, Heinkel had a no-hitter, striking out six in the Shockers' 11-6 victory. "I didn't deserve it," Heinkel admitted. "But I'll take it. I was fighting myself all the way until the fifth, when I said, 'Relax.' "

NCAA team records set in 1979
Batting average (.384)
Runs (828)
RBIs (714)
Total bases (1,506)
Slugging pct. (.625)
Doubles (181)
Extra-base hits (333)
Wins (65)

WSU's original 1979 schedule had 93 games, but some were lost to weather or cancellations.

Mike Davis took over well for Bob Bomerito at third base.

Don Heinkel was a crafty pitcher with a durable arm.

There was barely enough room in the Mathewson Junior High gym for the Shockers to play catch, let alone practice.

CRACKERBOX PRACTICES Early season workouts were always interesting for Stephenson's teams. Usually, with cold and wet weather in February and early March, the Shockers were forced inside. But where?

Relief came at the old Mathewson Junior High building, a block from campus at 18th and Chautauqua. The school's gym was small, but at least it was indoors and dry.

"Man, it's tiny," Stephenson once said. "It's tough to even throw in here. But it's better than nothing at all, and that's exactly what we'd have if we went back to Wichita State University."

ALOHA, MOTHER NATURE Hampered again and again by rain in Wichita, the 1980 opener was moved all the way to Hawaii. It was the first trip in what has become a semi-annual excursion for WSU.

Stephenson looked at the first trip as a way of saying thanks to the original players who joined the program and stuck with it. Ten juniors made up that group. "But if all I cared about were sunshine and warm weather," Stephenson quipped, "we could have opened in Edinburg, Texas."

Playing 10 games, the Shockers went 7-2-1, and that included taking 3 of 4 from No. 6 Hawaii.

WE'RE ALL WINNERS WSU had already taken the first four games from Hawaii-Hilo when it must have felt it coming from all sides in Game 5. With the score tied at 5 and the bases loaded with Shockers in the top of the ninth and nobody out, rain began to fall and the umpires delayed the game.

18. Who set the Shocker record of 30 2/3 consecutive scoreless innings?

But the Hilo grounds crew made no effort to cover the field, so WSU players rushed out and pulled the tarp on the field. When the rain stopped, the umpire walked out onto the tarp and called the game without looking underneath.

WSU's players rushed the umpire as Stephenson pleaded

THE CONFIDENT JOE CARTER

Before he was regularly driving in 100 runs in the majors, Joe Carter was a 6-foot-3, 195-pound kid from Oklahoma City with a ton of raw talent for baseball.

He had played third base, shortstop and even pitched in high school, all while hitting an amazing .833 his senior year. When he arrived at WSU, though, Stephenson told Carter he was an outfielder.

"The scouts who saw him in high school thought he was too raw, too rough and too inexperienced to be a pro prospect," Stephenson said. "I knew he would be a great player, but I didn't know how long it would take."

Not long. Carter began and ended his career as the greatest hitter in Shocker history. He hit .430 for his three-year career, still tops in Shocker record books. His .788 slugging percentage remains a school best, too. So that means that Carter, a three-time first-team All-American and the 1981 Player of the Year, was the best hitter AND power hitter in WSU history.

"I have confidence in my ability to hit," Carter told the Wichita Eagle-Beacon in 1981. "If I didn't, I might as well take three strikes and go out to play the field."

Yeah, that happened often. Carter's career continued in the pros, after he was the second overall pick by the Chicago Cubs in June 1981. His major-league career has had many turns. From Chicago to Cleveland to San Diego to Toronto, Carter has been a bit of a hitting nomad: Have bat, will travel.

But his home run against Mitch Williams in Game 6 of the 1993 World Series will stand as one of the most memorable moments

Joe Carter hit .430 during his three-year career.

in baseball history. Skipping around the bases with a smile and a boyishness that WSU fans remember brought an unmistakable warmth to every Shocker fan's heart.

That was, after all, OUR Joe.

WSU was 7-1 in the MVC's Western Division in 1980, winning the conference tourney at home and earning an NCAA bid.

with the Hilo coach to continue the game. When the coach finally agreed, play was about to resume when the Hilo coach came rushing to the plate to confer with the ump.

The ump called the game again, this time for good. The Hilo coach, not admitting that his team was about to be beaten, said he was worried for his players' safety on the wet field.

The punchline? The Shockers picked up a Honolulu newspaper the next day to find out they had lost the game 5-4.

BREAKING IN BASES One of WSU's bigger routs came in March 1980, when the Shockers scored 53 runs in a doubleheader blitz of Augustana College. But the games almost weren't played.

WSU went two full seasons without being shut out, until the 1981 opener against NAIA champion Grand Canyon.

When the Shockers arrived to prepare their field for the game, they found the diamond's lock had been broken and the bases had been stolen, with beer cans left on the pitcher's mound. WSU had to scramble around town to find new bases in time for the first pitch. Unfortunately for Augustana, they arrived.

ASTOUNDING STATS As would become custom, WSU continually put a hurt on its record books and the NCAA's, too. By the end of the 1980 season, four Shockers (Davis, Carter, Phil Stephenson, Bomerito) hit .400.

Joe Carter and Phil Stephenson were both first-team All-America in 1981.

More impressively, Stephenson set an NCAA record with 104 runs, and Carter did the same with 34 doubles and 229 total bases. Stephenson also stole 42 bases in 43 tries.

Even crazier, Don Heinkel had maybe the single-best pitching season in NCAA history. In 17 starts, he compiled a 14-3 record with 12 complete games and an unheard-of 1.74 ERA. The length of his average outing was 7 1/3 innings, which could have been higher if some of his starts had not been in seven-inning games.

Seven Shockers were first-team All-Valley in 1980.

"Don is the epitome of what a pitcher should be," Stephenson said. "He is a real bulldog and has a purpose with every pitch."

SUMMERTIME BLUES Jim Thomas, WSU's second baseman of the future, found himself tumbling over a player sliding into second base with a half-roll block, half-slide during a summer league game in Boulder, Colo.

Thomas suffered torn ligaments in his knee and was done for the summer. Thomas felt terribly, but so did the guy who slid into second: WSU teammate Keith "Spider" Jones, who played for Macy's Diesels of Rapid City, S.D. Thomas was ready by the Shocker opener in 1981.

Jim Thomas always gave everything he had in baseball.

PHIL'S SUPER STRING It started in early March, during a no-surprise 10-0 rout of Marymount. Phil Stephenson got a hit, no big deal.

Next game, he got another. And so on, and so on. Over the next 47 games, Stephenson would have a stretch of hitting that most players only fantasize about. He got a hit in each of those games, setting an NCAA record for consecutive games with a hit.

This was no one-hit-per-night thing, either. Stephenson, who was moved by his brother Gene from leadoff into the third spot to take advantage of his power, saw his average climb above .500 at times during the string.

Finally, in a 9-4 loss to Oklahoma State, Stephenson's streak ended. He grounded out, fouled out, had a sacrifice fly and lined out. "I knew this day would come," Stephenson said. "I didn't know it would come quite this soon."

WILD DAY IN OMAHA The craziest game of the 1981 season was the second game of a double-header against Creighton. The game took 4 hours, 16 minutes and included:

■ Ten home runs, which included Carter's blast that made him the NCAA career leader.

■ Seven errors, a triple play and 11 stolen bases (six from Stephenson alone).

■ Terry Hayes' pitching line: five innings, 12 hits, 14 runs (only 11 earned), seven walks, four strikeouts.

■ A seven-run eighth inning by Creighton, which helped the Bluejays win a 23-22 thriller.

The funny thing? WSU won the first game 3-1 in a game that took less than half the time as Game 2.

Phil Stephenson found all the holes in 1981.

The '81 braintrust: Terry Jolly, Gene Stephenson and Brent Kemnitz.

1982: TASTE OF THE FUTURE

The 1982 Shockers were 4-6 after their first 10 games, 69-8 from there.

Six hard-hitting seniors were done after the 1981 season, and it looked as though three outstanding juniors – Carter, Stephenson and Thomas – would be high draft picks and turn pro. It was going to be Gene Stephenson's toughest rebuilding job to date.

But he would get help. Phil Stephenson and Thomas both stayed at WSU, though the three-time All-America Carter opted to sign with the Chicago Cubs. Carter, one of seven Shockers to sign in 1981, was the No. 2 overall

A HIT EVERY TIME

You can toss out statistic after statistic to prove what a great college baseball player Phil Stephenson was. In his four-year career at WSU, his name was

Phil Stephenson is still the NCAA career stolen-base leader.

among the leaders in nearly every category of NCAA records.

But nothing gets to the heart of Stephenson like this: There were several games in the middle of the 1981 season where a 2-for-4 day would knock Stephenson's average DOWN.

It's amazing to think a player would have a 50 percent chance of getting a hit each time he was at bat, but that's the kind of season Stephenson had in 1981. He didn't finish there – a "disappointing" .447 was the final number – but he did set an NCAA mark for consecutive games with a hit (47).

"Someday this streak will stop," Stephenson said the day he broke the old record at 45. "And when it

does, I'll just start another one."

Classic Phil Stephenson. His average at-bat included a sweet swing, followed by a hit somewhere to the outfield. But Stephenson's game didn't end there. He was also the most prolific base stealer in NCAA history, swiping an amazing 206 out of 221. That's a 93.2 percent success rate.

"He makes everything look so easy," his brother Gene once said. "He's the kind of player that has to grow on you."

But success was standard for Stephenson, who proved himself as more than just Gene's brother when he stepped on campus in 1978. His freshman season, he hit a mere .443. Even today, he still holds NCAA marks for career hits (418), runs (420), total bases (730), stolen bases (206) and walks (300). Adding his total bases, stolen bases and walks, Stephenson alone accounted for 1,206 bases. That's 300.2 per season or 4.2 per game.

"My theory about hitting is that every time I go to the plate, I feel like I'll get one good pitch to hit well," Stephenson said. "It's very seldom that that doesn't happen."

pick in the 1981 draft and a month later was hitting .300 at Double-A Midland.

Even with Carter gone, there were still plenty of studs at Shocker Field.

ROLLING TOWARD THE TOURNEYS Nobody in the Valley touched WSU, either during the season or in the postseason tournament. The Shockers actually got better competition with a few tough regular-season games near the end.

First, WSU knocked off ninth-ranked Oklahoma State 8-3. Then just before the tournament, the Shockers turned back visiting Arizona State (the No. 1-ranked bunch that swept WSU in March) in 2 of 3 games at Lawrence-Dumont Stadium. ASU coach Jim Brock said afterward, "If they're not one of the five best teams in the country, then I'm not a major college coach."

Taking 2 of 3 from third-ranked Cal State-Fullerton after the Valley Tournament had WSU ranked as high as No. 4 and primed for the South Regional in New Orleans.

MARDI GRAS IN MAY There was no team better set up for a regional than Wichita State. When you have three starting pitchers of All-America status, it's tough to top.

Heinkel got the call in Game 1 of the South Regional, shutting out Jackson State 3-0. Oelkers followed with a 7-0 shutout of host New Orleans, then Sonberg put the Privateers away again in the final, giving up no runs over seven innings for an 8-1 triumph and a berth in the College World Series. For the regional, the three starters combined to throw 26 consecutive scoreless innings, giving up only 10 hits in that stretch.

Charlie O'Brien hit .600 and was named the regional MVP, but it's hard to argue with the starters combining for that honor.

"Never have I seen two lefties like the ones on that team," New Orleans shortstop Augie Schmidt said of Oelkers and Sonberg. "That's the best team we've played in my three years here. They've definitely got a shot to go all the way."

In Stephenson's fifth season, his boys would get their chance.

ON THE RIGHT TRACK The Shockers knew pitching was the key, and Oelkers delivered in the CWS opener. Facing a familiar Cal State-Fullerton team, he fired a five-hit shutout for a 7-0 victory.

But three nights later, Heinkel had problems with Miami. The Hurricanes roughed up the Shocker right-hander with three solo home runs in a 4-3 victory, sending WSU to the loser's bracket.

But that game will forever be known for more than solo homers.

Erik Sonberg was a future first-round pick by the Dodgers.

19. Who beat WSU for the Shockers' only Valley loss in 1982?

Don Heinkel, Brian Oelkers, above, and Erik Sonberg were the most feared trio of pitchers in the country.

Gene Stephenson joked WSU was "just coming (to Omaha) for the party."

THE PHANTOM PICKOFF Not a College World Series goes by without ESPN showing The Play over again. When it happened, it was a clever play that got Miami out of a jam in its 4-3 win over Wichita State. Today, it's some pretty good humor.

With record-setting base stealer Phil Stephenson on first and dusk settling in at Rosenblatt Stadium, Miami pitcher Mike Kasprzak wheeled to first yet another time. As Stephenson dived back, first baseman Steve Lusby dived after the wild throw, which traveled all the way to the Miami bullpen, where the relief pitchers and ballgirls scrambled to get out of the way.

Only the throw was never made. Kasprzak kept the ball, while Stephenson looked for the ball, assumed it was well away from first base, and took off for second. As he hustled to second, Kasprzak calmly threw to short-stop Bill Wrona, who tagged the surprised Stephenson for the inning-ending out.

Several factors helped the play. At twilight, the pitcher was hard to see from first base. Miami's bullpen and ball-girls did a great job of acting, as did the dugout and Lusby at first base. And it didn't help that Shocker pitcher Bryan Oelkers, who that day had been the No. 4 overall pick in the pro draft, was coaching first base.

You had to see it to believe it. And if you haven't seen it, just watch the CWS on TV next year. It'll be on eventually.

THROUGH THE BACK DOOR Knocked into the loser's bracket, WSU began the long road back by sending 10 men to the plate in the first inning, scoring five times in a 13-2 rout of Oklahoma State. Hibbs was 4 for 5, Morman 3 for 6 with six RBIs and his 22nd homer, and Sonberg struck out 13 'Pokes.

Two nights later, with a berth in the championship game at stake, the Shockers disposed of Texas All-American Calvin Schiraldi in an 8-4 victory. Oelkers threw a complete game and the Shocker bats punished Schiraldi for seven runs, seven hits and three walks in 2 2/3 innings.

A rematch with Miami was next, but there was a cost.

Kevin Penner's career would be changed by Calvin Schiraldi's fastball.

THE SCARIEST MOMENT The pitch headed straight for Kevin Penner's face, and he couldn't get out of the way. Schiraldi's fastball struck the sophomore outfielder just below the left eye and shattered his cheekbone, lodging a piece of bone against the eye.

Doctors at University Hospital in Ann Arbor, Mich., took bone from Penner's skull to rebuild the foundation of the eye socket. There was no nerve damage, but Penner's vision was blurred and it was thought his baseball career was over.

But before fall practice in 1982, Penner's vision improved and he was back on the field, although this time with a facemask on his helmet. "All summer long, I just sat and watched baseball games on TV," Penner said. "It never occurred to me that I'd be playing again. But by the end of the summer, I was getting fired up."

ANOTHER SHOT AT THE CANES A two-run first inning, followed by Morman's mammoth homer in the third, gave WSU a 3-0 lead through four innings. With Heinkel on the mound, it had to be a safe lead, right?

Not against Miami. The Hurricanes put up six runs in the fifth, and they allowed only two more hits the rest of the way in a 9-3 championship victory.

Regardless of the final loss, it was WSU's finest season. The Shockers finished 73-14 – 73 wins is still an NCAA record – and lost only eight times in the final three months. Phil Stephenson was named national Player of the Year, Gene Stephenson was national Coach of the Year, four players were first-team All-America (Stephenson, Oelkers, Heinkel and O'Brien), and three players were on the second or third teams (Morman, Sonberg and Thomas).

"I'm proud as I can be of our players, and I think we really put our program on the map," Stephenson said. "I think we gave a good accounting of ourselves. Shocker fans should be proud."

'NUFF SAID WSU was 43-9 and ranked second when Nebraska visited Shocker Field on April 30. The Cornhuskers won 12-3, snapping the Shocks' 49-game home winning streak.

Stephenson said only, "I have no comment. None."

MORMAN'S MAMMOTHS Sure, there have been some great power hitters in Shocker history. Carter, Standiford, Davis, O'Brien and Davis are just a few.

Russ Morman was as good as any of 'em. Overshadowed slightly because he played only two seasons at WSU, Morman's name is still a frequent sight in the Shocker record book.

He hit more homers per at-bat (one every 12.1 times up), was No. 2 in slugging percentage, No. 5 in home runs, and still hit .406 for his career. Project his two-year figures over a three- or four-year career and Morman would easily be tops in most power categories.

WE'RE NO. 1, BUT ... Respect was tough for WSU to earn in the first years of its rebirth. But on May 10, 1983, the Shockers moved up to No. 1 in Collegiate Baseball's poll,

20. What strange occurrence happened at the end of WSU's loss to Miami in the national championship game?

Bryan Oelkers, Don Heinkel and Erik Sonberg combined for a 51-10 record in 1982, with ERAs ranging from 2.07 to 2.23.

Gene Stephenson turned down an offer of managing and being a Class-A general manager in the Mets organization.

Russ Morman hit 47 homers in two seasons.

QUIZ

21. Who hit the first home run once Shocker Field's name was changed to Eck Stadium?

the first time WSU owned the top spot (Baseball America ranked WSU first briefly in 1982, but the magazine wasn't widely circulated then).

But three days after becoming the new No. 1, Wichita State lost five of its next seven games, including 2 of 3 in the Valley Tournament and 3 of 4 to visiting Pan American.

The slide continued in the Midwest Regional at Stillwater. WSU lost to Oklahoma State, rebounded briefly with a 6-3 win over Arkansas, then was eliminated by Oral Roberts 6-5. "We just didn't have the horses to win this thing," Stephenson said.

FINALLY, A STADIUM Ted Bredehoft never delivered on his promise of a first-class baseball facility at Wichita State. When he resigned late in 1982, there were still portable toilets, portable stands and no other amenities.

But on Dec. 16, 1983, the Kansas Board of Regents approved a half-million dollar stadium to be built around Shocker Field. All funds would come from private donations, but it was the first real move toward a stadium that fit the needs of a first-class program.

"This has been a long time coming," Stephenson said,

"but I think it's something most people believe we've earned and need. We're thrilled."

By the time the 1985 season rolled around, the Shockers were playing in Eck Stadium, named after local car dealer Rusty Eck, who donated about 30 percent of the money for the $700,000 project.

THE POST-MONSTER ERA

With mashers such as Carter, Stephenson, Morman and O'Brien gone, the Shocker teams of the mid-1980s found success a little tougher to come by.

Not that the 40-22 record of 1984 was chopped liver, but it was the lowest winning percentage (.645) of any Stephenson team since the first year. That club, as well as the 1986 team that went 45-18, was shut out of the NCAA Tournament.

But there were signs that a resurgence was coming.

STUB STANDS IN How could a guy only 5-foot-7 and 160 pounds hit as many home runs as Mark Standiford did in his four years at Wichita State?

"He's got fast hands, and he's a strong kid, too," Stephenson said of Standiford during his freshman season. "The best thing is he has great quickness in his hands, which generates a lot of power."

Mark Standiford had an outstanding power stroke for a little man.

Stepping in as the Shockers' second baseman after a standout career at Wichita North High, Standiford immediately became the cornerstone of WSU's power supply. He hit a team-best 16 homers as a freshman and eventually became the school's home-run champ with 69, 11 more than Carter.

CHECKING IN AT ECK The first part of the 1985 home schedule was played at Lawrence-Dumont Stadium, while the finishing touches were being put on renovations to Shocker Field.

On April 11, though, Eck Stadium opened for business with a Shocker sweep of Kansas Newman. "It's good to be home," Penner said. "We've been waiting for this day a long time."

The stadium featured 3,407 permanent seats, bathrooms, locker rooms, concession stands and offices for the baseball staff. Ten years later, it seemed primitive, but considering the situation seven years earlier, it was a shrine to Stephenson's program.

"It's hard not to come up here without tears in your eyes," Stephenson said after Game 1 in Eck. "I think about all the efforts of a lot of people and players and the things we've gone through."

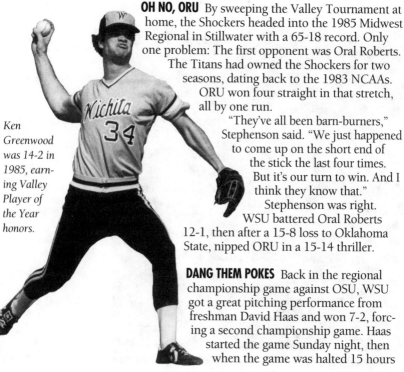

Ken Greenwood was 14-2 in 1985, earning Valley Player of the Year honors.

OH NO, ORU By sweeping the Valley Tournament at home, the Shockers headed into the 1985 Midwest Regional in Stillwater with a 65-18 record. Only one problem: The first opponent was Oral Roberts. The Titans had owned the Shockers for two seasons, dating back to the 1983 NCAAs. ORU won four straight in that stretch, all by one run.

"They've all been barn-burners," Stephenson said. "We just happened to come up on the short end of the stick the last four times. But it's our turn to win. And I think they know that."

Stephenson was right. WSU battered Oral Roberts 12-1, then after a 15-8 loss to Oklahoma State, nipped ORU in a 15-14 thriller.

DANG THEM POKES Back in the regional championship game against OSU, WSU got a great pitching performance from freshman David Haas and won 7-2, forcing a second championship game. Haas started the game Sunday night, then when the game was halted 15 hours by rain, came back the next day and kept pitching.

The most interesting thing about the weekend was the strategy the Shockers had for Pete Incaviglia, the Cowboys' slugger. After he homered to tie the first game at 2, WSU proceeded to intentionally walk him seven consecutive times. Twice, with nobody on base.

"Emotionally, that takes a lot out of them to get their best hitter out of the game," Haas said. "We didn't want to let him beat us."

But some other Pokes stepped up and Oklahoma State won 10-6. Said OSU coach Gary Ward: "That ballclub (WSU) would win half of the regionals in this country."

Gene Stephenson's 500th win came on the second day of the 1987 season. He joined Texas' Cliff Gustafson and Arizona State's Jim Brock as the only coaches to win 500 games in 10 seasons.

INJURY BUG'S TARGET When Tim Raley was involved in a car accident in January 1986, it looked as if he would miss much, if not all, of the upcoming season.

But that wasn't Raley's style. A knee ligament injury wasn't going to stop him from playing in 61 of the Shockers' 63 games, and hitting a team-best .387 with 11 homers and 71 RBIs. Raley was used to injuries, having missed part of the 1985 postseason with a broken right arm.

When Raley was healthy, though, he was one of the school's most consistent hitters. His left-handed stroke put together averages of .384, .386, .387 and, in his senior year, .412. A four-year starter in left field, Raley hit .394 for his career and trailed only Phil Stephenson and Jim Thomas on the career hits chart. Raley also is in the Shocker top five in runs, doubles, triples, RBIs, total bases and walks.

"It's very difficult to pitch to him with any type of consistency," Stephenson said during Raley's senior year. "Just when you think you have him figured out, he'll hammer you. He's smart. He's very smart."

WSU's 45-18 mark in 1986 was a down year since the Shocks didn't win the Valley regular season for only the second time in Stephenson's first eight years.

After a 29-year baseball hiatus, Kansas and WSU finally met again in 1986. WSU scored 15 runs in the seventh inning for a 18-6 victory.

HAMMER TIME The first eight Shockers reached base without an out, so there were surely signs that the game with Kansas Wesleyan wasn't going to be pretty.

Seven merciless innings later – mercy came when the game was called because of the landslide – WSU had posted a 35-0 victory. Every Shocker was hot, but DH Rick Olivas was the hottest: He hit for the cycle, drove in seven runs and scored a record six himself.

Freshman pitcher Craig Marshall, given a 35-run lead, didn't falter. His biggest problem was keeping his arm loose while his teammates were batting for 30 or 40 minutes at a time.

Even in 1987, baseball wasn't a great draw. The Shockers averaged less than 600 fans per home game.

CALIFORNIA DAY DREAMIN' Sent west for the NCAA Tournament, the Shockers found themselves in Palo Alto, Calif., where they beat Cal-Santa Barbara 4-3 in the first round. In Game 2, WSU had a 3-2 lead over another

Tim Raley (3) was as consistent a hitter as WSU had seen.

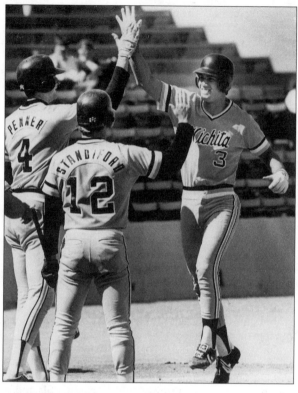

Backup shortstop Mike Blankenberger had the two biggest hits in WSU's 1987 conference tournament victory.

Ron Tyler went from Shocker starter to Shocker supporter.

WSU – Washington State – in the ninth inning.

Usually, that meant the game was over. WSU hadn't lost a lead in the final inning all season.

But the Cougars scored two in the ninth and won 4-3 over a WSU team that had just seven singles. The team's only RBIs were on two sacrifice flies and a bases-loaded walk. "I don't understand how come we're not swinging the bats any better than this," Stephenson said after the game. "I thought we would come out today and play with a lot more confidence."

It didn't happen the next day, either. WSU was 4-0 on the season against Oral Roberts, but the Titans beat WSU 11-4 to end the Shockers' season at 59-20.

TYLER FIELD Ron Tyler was a pitcher for Wichita State in the 1960s, though he'd be the first to admit he wasn't one of the school's all-time greats.

But Tyler made his mark on the Shocker baseball program in another way in 1988, when he announced he and his wife, Linda, were forming a $4.425 million trust for the program. Tyler, co-founder of Residence Inns, helped WSU fund two more scholarships, reaching the NCAA maximum of 13, and improve many areas of the ballpark.

Among the improvements: new artificial turf, a rubberized warning track, a cedar outfield fence, five sections of box seats directly behind the backstop, and a new public-address system.

"This is more than 'great' from my standpoint," Stephenson said. "This is just awesome."

ONE TOUGH HAAS Haas came back for his senior season in 1988 with something to prove. After his junior season,

AN ITCH TO COMPETE

Early in the 1989 season, Gene Stephenson was on a recruiting trip and found himself stranded in Denver's Stapleton Airport because of a snowstorm. That afternoon, his Shockers were at home ready to face Texas Christian.

It would have been easy to wait it out in Denver. After all, his 10th-ranked team would surely pulverize TCU.

But the only thing that Stephenson hates more than losing is not playing at all. He caught a private flight and headed home, flying over the stadium 25 minutes after the first pitch. When he started putting on his uniform, it was the bottom of the second in a 1-1 game. WSU won 16-2, of course.

Fiery. Competitive. Emotional. Gutty. All those describe the man who took Shocker baseball out of the grave and into the collegiate spotlight.

"…The positive thing is that we never go into a game here thinking we're going to lose," said pitching coach Brent Kemnitz, at Stephenson's side for all but the first year. "I don't care who we're playing, whether it's home or away. That attitude comes from the top."

That attitude has accounted for 1,004 wins in 18 seasons, a .762 winning percentage and conference

Whether it's tiddlywinks or baseball, Gene Stephenson is there to win.

championships in 13 of the 15 years WSU has competed in the Valley. It has brought six College World Series appearances, four championship games and the unforgettable 1989 march to the pinnacle.

His players, whether they agreed to join WSU while looking at a bare spot of grass or a multi-million dollar stadium, have always followed his lead: Hustle, commitment and work ethic bring results.

Gene Stephenson will have nothing less.

"The only way I'd ever be content, I guess, is if we won them all and the players were perfect in every game," Stephenson said. "That ain't gonna happen."

David Haas was the anchor of a deep 1988 pitching staff.

WSU more than doubled its previous attendance best when 5,126 fans saw WSU fall to Oklahoma State in 1988.

Dan Raley finally made the CWS in 1988.

when he went 15-2 and upped his career record to an incredible 35-5, he was drafted by Toronto and forgotten about. No signing bonus, no negotiations, just a letter and single contract offer.

No way. Haas was back at WSU to be the heart of a deep pitching staff. Along with Greg Brummett, Shane Durham, Pat Cedeno and Jim Newlin, the Shockers had their best staff since the early '80s.

Haas had earned his spot as the most dependable starter. Besides sparkling in the Midwest Regional his freshman year, he won 10 straight games before suffering his first loss. As a junior, he was a third-team All-America, All-Valley for the second straight time, and won a nation's-best 15 games (including consecutive four-hit shutouts in Hawaii).

HE MAY BE RIGHT An early season winning streak of 15 games in 1988 included a three-game sweep of No. 7 LSU at Lawrence-Dumont Stadium. Avenging a three-game sweep at Baton Rouge in 1987, WSU won this time 5-3, 5-3 and 13-0.

By April, renovations to Eck Stadium were done and the park was ready for its boys again. The Shockers won their first dozen games back there, including an 8-3 win over Nebraska that included three home runs from Standiford. A week later, the not-so-fleet-footed Dan Raley legged out an inside-the-park homer in the ninth to beat ORU 7-6.

VALLEY OF COMEBACKS Halfway through the second weekend of conference play, WSU stood 2-4 and looked sunk in the standings. But the Shockers won the final two at Illinois State, then swept four-game series at home with Bradley and Southern Illinois.

It would come down to a four-game series at Creighton for the Valley regular-season crown. Both teams were 12-4.

WSU won the opener 7-6 on Jeff Bonacquista's single in the ninth, then took the second game 19-5 with five home runs.

On Sunday, the road to Omaha actually started in Omaha. Trailing 3-1 in the ninth inning of the opener and with nobody on and two outs, WSU scored five times to stun the Bluejays and capture the Valley crown.

Oh, by the way, it was Stephenson's 600th career victory, a milestone he would remember. WSU won the second game, too, finishing with a league-record 16-4 mark.

RAILING ON RALEY If Dan Raley wore his emotions on his sleeve, his sleeve would be the size of Montana. During his Shocker career, he did everything from punching a concrete wall to kicking benches to slamming helmets to verbally assaulting himself.

But in hitting a team-best .384 his senior season, Raley learned to channel his emotions from assaulting innocent objects to assaulting the baseball.

"I have calmed down a lot, believe me, since my freshman year," Raley told The Eagle-Beacon in 1988. "It took me three years to figure it out. This is supposed to be fun."

Raley hit in 29 of 33 games during a 1988 stretch and is among the Shockers' top six career leaders in doubles (61), RBIs (242) and walks (235).

Shocker first baseman Mike McDonald improved his average 60 points in less than two months during the '88 season.

ONE CRAZY TOURNEY The 1988 Valley Tournament will be remembered as much for what didn't happen as for what did. The Shockers were 3-0 and in the tourney final against Creighton, a team it had already beaten.

Tied at 3 in the eighth inning, rain poured on the stadium for the remainder of the night and next morning. That became crucial when the NCAA selection committee informed the conference that it could only assure the MVC one spot in the regionals and not two.

Conditions never improved, so Wichita State was declared the champion and got the automatic berth based on its regular-season championship. That deprived Creighton an NCAA berth, even though the Bluejays were 43-21 with victories over two NCAA-bound teams.

Shane Durham and Pat Cedeno pitched WSU into the College World Series, beating OSU twice to win the 1988 regional.

"It was complete devastation and the ultimate disappointment for the players," CU coach Jim Hendry said. "They feel they were deprived of something that was rightfully theirs."

AMERICA'S TEAM Once in Omaha, the Shockers quickly gained the title of home team, since they were the only kids from the Midwest. Eagle-Beacon columnist Fred Mann said it best:

"WSU players are the only guys in the Series who need to use sun lamps in the winter. They are solid midwestern kids. They don't drive to work in Mercedes or get summer jobs unloading cocaine from ships in Miami harbor. None of the Shocks have worked as extras in a movie, or traveled with the Brat Pack."

No, they were from the Plains, and the people of Omaha and Rosenblatt Stadium quickly took to them in WSU's 5-4 opening-game win over Florida. "This team throughout the year has had one thing in mind, and that's being No. 1," starter David Haas said afterward. "We know we're not going to get a lot of recognition, so we gotta go out and beat teams."

ROUND 1 WSU spotted Arizona State three unearned runs in a second-round game, only to have pitcher Greg Brummett dominate the Sun Devils from there.

The Shockers won 7-4 and were one win away from the title game.

An unsung hero in that game was Dan Raley, but not for his performance in the game. Before the game, Raley threw batting-practice pitches to two-thirds of his teammates in a style that ASU pitcher Linty Ingram used. It worked, too, as WSU beat the nation's top-ranked team.

THE FATEFUL ROUND 2 Arizona State worked its way through the loser's bracket for another shot at WSU. But Haas was sharp for eight innings, holding down a six-hitter and a 3-1 lead with two outs and a runner on second.

Then came two of the bleakest pitches in Shocker history. Ahead 0-2 on Ricky Candelari, Haas made a mistake and Candelari singled home the run to make it 3-2.

Haas gave up another single, putting runners on first and second with two outs. Again, he got ahead 0-2 on Pat Listach, who was 0 for 4 with three strikeouts.

But again, the Sun Devils got the hit. Listach singled to left on a hanging curve to score the tying run. Haas was taken out for Jim Newlin, who got the last out in the ninth but gave up a 10th-inning run for the 4-3 loss. The two teams would meet again in two days for a berth in the championship game.

"We let some two-strike pitches get away from us," Stephenson said, "and I made a mistake. I just went too long with (Haas). I'll say it."

But Haas shouldered the blame. "He says it was his fault, but it was my fault. You've got to rise to the occasion. It came down to getting the last out, and three times in a row they got base hits on me."

Unable to get over the sudden loss, WSU lost to ASU 19-1 two days later.

A FAIRY TALE COMES TRUE

The story of the 1989 Wichita State baseball season ends with glory, a national championship trophy, playing some catch at the White House and a warm fuzzy feeling inside for all Shocker fans.

But before all that, came some of the most unbelievable stories WSU athletics has ever seen. Injury after injury, setback after setback. This team couldn't go on, could it? There was too much keeping them from succeeding.

Except for pride. Determination. A competitive fire that came from the top and went all the way to the student trainers. The '89 Shockers were labeled the "Back to the Wall Gang." Amazing how guys with backs to the wall could break through so many other barriers.

If you're a Shocker fan, you'll never forget where you were in mid-afternoon on June 10, 1989. You'll never forget Bryant Winslow coming off the field, Pat Meares' sweet home-run swing, Greg Brummett's icy stare toward the

plate or Gene Stephenson holding up the trophy.

Champions.

MISSING INGREDIENT Seems funny now, but the big question mark when the Shockers began workouts in the winter of 1989 was the team's heart. Hitting, pitching and defense were already in place. Guts weren't.

"I think chemistry is going to be a big factor," catcher Eric Wedge said. "The attitude of this team has yet to be seen."

WELCOME, GEORGIA, BRR, TECH WSU was riding a 17-game winning streak when Georgia Tech visited Eck Stadium in mid-March for a two-game series to be televised on ESPN. The Yellow Jackets realized they had left the Sun Belt when they arrived.

WSU won the opener 13-2, getting a big homer from Mike McDonald – "From that point on, I think you could probably almost hear the TVs clicking off around the country," Stephenson said. The next day, it was so cold that the attendance was announced at 70 but really only 10 by the final inning.

Greg Brummett and Eric Wedge embrace after winning the national championship.

Eric Wedge was one of the team's emotional leaders.

The Shockers got warm in Hawaii, though, winning the Rainbow Easter Tournament the next week, but their school-record winning streak of 24 games was ended by Hawaii. Brummett took the loss to the Rainbows. He wouldn't lose again in 1989.

A recommendation to scout Pat Meares was crucial to WSU's success.

THANKS, BLUE Sacred Heart High School in Salina didn't have a baseball team, so Pat Meares played golf in the spring. Played it so well, in fact, that he won the 1986 Class 3-2-1A tournament.

But baseball was Meares' best sport. He was a standout in Salina's American Legion league, where Stephenson first saw his future center fielder-third baseman-shortstop.

How did Stephenson hear of Meares? From an umpire, Dennis Walker, who has worked Shocker games for years. Walker is from Salina, too, and worked many of Meares' Legion games.

WSU missed the arm of right fielder Jeff Bonacquista.

THE BUG BITES Jeff Bonacquista was a dependable hitter with a rocket arm in right field. Opposing baserunners knew better than to try him on a throw to the plate.

But it was a throw at the plate that ended Bonacquista's four-year career as a Shocker. Trying to score from third on a wild pitch, he was hit on the kneecap by a throw from Illinois State catcher Dan Prybylinski. The kneecap broke and Bonacquista's season was over.

"You know what you're going to get every day from a guy like him," said a saddened Stephenson. Stephenson didn't know who would be in right field the next week, saying, "Whoever it is, it's going to be a strange situation because, as far as game situations go, he's the only guy out there for four years."

THE BOTTOM DROPS There were down moments in 1989, to be sure. Stephenson felt his team gave up in an 11-6 home loss to Oklahoma State, and a 4-4 start in the conference wasn't ideal, either. But all that was soothing compared to the team's mood after a road trip to Bradley.

In all, WSU and Bradley met for only 15 innings (and two WSU wins) because of rain. But it was poor communication between Bradley and the Valley office that hampered efforts to get the games in. The Eagle-Beacon reported that conference associate commissioner Joe Mitch changed his mind four times about what to do during what was supposed to be a four-game series.

Stephenson blasted the Valley and the Braves. "As far as I'm concerned, they can have their league without Wichita State," Stephenson said. "We don't need to be in a league that doesn't want to compete on a national level. My recommendation would be that we pull out of this mess."

Counting the Peoria series, WSU won 9 of its last 10 Valley games for another regular-season title, but lost two games to Indiana State in the Valley Tournament.

THAT DAMN BUG AGAIN A chronic back problem had bothered shortstop Mike Lansing all season, and by the postseason it was too much for the second-team All-America to withstand. He would be out for the regional with a ruptured disc suffered in a batting practice.

A three-year starter at shortstop, Lansing was a spark plug in the Shockers' offense and a steady defensive player. With him out, Pat Meares moved from third to short, DH Mike Jones went to third and Mike Wentworth filled in as DH.

All that and more. Everybody knew that first baseman Bryant Winslow, a sophomore, was hobbling on a stress fracture in his right leg. "Each day, it seems to be getting a little bit worse," Stephenson said. "But he says he can hang on another week."

THE ROUGH ROAD Portland and Pepperdine were easy victims in the regional's first two rounds, but Michigan was

With another regional bid nailed down, WSU was named the top seed at Fresno, Calif.

The loss of Mike Lansing caused a huge lineup shakeup.

Mike Wentworth's place in Shocker baseball history is secure.

a toughie. The Wolverines won 14-5, putting WSU in an elimination game an hour later against hometown Fresno State and its 5,000 fans.

But the Shockers' magic was beginning. McDonald homered to get WSU within 4-3, then Wentworth hit his first homer of the season to give the Shockers a 5-4 lead they wouldn't give up. Wentworth was in the lineup only because the injury to Lansing forced a shift in the order.

How nice, Wentworth thought. He homered on his mom's birthday.

SMELLING OMAHA Michigan had whipped the Shockers days before, and now WSU had to win two straight to get back to the College World Series.

Darned if they didn't do it. Pat Cedeno and Jeff Bluma combined for a 3-2 win in the first game, then freshman Charlie Giaudrone, Bluma and closer Jim Newlin allowed only three earned runs in the 9-5 nightcap.

Never the easy way, only the right way.

"Don't ever count these guys out," Stephenson said. "Too many people try to scratch us off and say it can't be done. But you can't ever count these guys out."

Were truer words ever spoken?

TIME FOR A CHANGE Sandwiched between two victories that eliminated Arkansas was a big loss to Florida State in the second round of the CWS. The Seminoles' Clyde Keller held the Shockers down most of the game in a 4-2 win.

Batting Mike McDonald third was one of the key changes in the Shocker order during the CWS.

With the offense struggling to a .221 average, Stephenson made some adjustments. He moved Wedge back to his comfortable cleanup role, putting McDonald ahead of him in hopes that he would see better pitches. Then Meares was moved up from ninth to sixth, one behind Winslow.

After the second win over Arkansas, which set up a scenario in which the Shockers had to beat FSU twice to get to the championship game, Stephenson was asked about his team's chances.

They didn't look any better than before, and maybe a bit worse. Center fielder Jim Audley had to leave Game 3 with a sprained ankle and was doubtful for Florida State, plus Wedge was nursing a bruised left forearm.

"No, we won't have nine healthy people to put out there," Stephenson said. "But I'll tell you one thing, they won't quit."

NO QUIT HERE After a 54-minute rain delay, Wedge hit an eighth-inning single into center that scored two runs and gave WSU the lead for good in a 7-4 win over the Seminoles, forcing another game for the right to play in the national title game against Texas.

FSU took the lead 4-1 in Game 2 before the most unlikely of heroes appeared again. Wentworth had already suffered at the plate, failing to move runners to second and third on a sacrifice try. He was playing only because Joey Wilson was 1 for 12 in the DH role over the three previous games.

But Wentworth connected. Again. With two men on, Wentworth rocketed a Keller mistake for a game-tying home run. WSU won a slugfest from there, outscoring FSU 8-5 from the sixth inning on to get into the CWS final.

Wentworth's second homer of the season came on his dad's birthday. Hmm. Then he revealed Wichita's Most Famous Fortune Ever to Come From Bazooka Bubble Gum, which he had opened before the game:

"Something magical will happen to you today."

ONE MORE During Greg Brummett's four-year career at Wichita State, his nickname was changed from "Fifi" to "Spike." Pretty obvious it had to do with his aggressiveness and tenacity as a pitcher.

So with nine innings standing between WSU and its first national championship, who better to take the ball? After all, Brummett was 17-2 on the season and would earn second-team All-America honors. Plus, he was already 2-0 in the tournament and wouldn't be strained working on three days' rest.

The fire in Greg Brummett's eyes showed for every pitch of the '89 title game.

There was first-inning trouble. A walk and single put runners on first and third with nobody out. But that's when Spike got tough. He faked a move to third and looked back to first, nailing David Tollison for the out.

"They had gained some confidence and I lost some confidence after those first two hitters," Brummett said. "Then I got the pickoff and right then and there, it gave me all the confidence in the world."

Brummett then struck out Scott Bryant and Arthur Butcher to get out of the inning. He sprinted off the field with an electric charge in him.

FIRST STRIKE Texas coach Cliff Gustafson decided on starting Bryant, a pitcher-DH who was the Collegiate Baseball Player of the Year. But it was only Bryant's fifth start, and none had been recently.

WSU made Gustafson pay for the risk. Three walks, a single and a wild pitch scored the game's first run and loaded the bases with two outs. That got Bryant pulled, but Todd Dreifort grounded out to end the inning.

WSU made it 3-0 in the second on two errors by Texas third baseman Scott Newkirk, but it was far from over.

UNFORGETTABLE FIFTH The big inning started with Winslow's agonizing leg injury. Realizing he wasn't help-

'DON'T YOU DARE LOSE THIS GAME'

His face was a mix of pure dirt and tears, his cap and uniform a complete mess. But Bryant Winslow wasn't coming out.

He couldn't walk, but he wasn't coming out. For weeks, Winslow had been hobbling around on his right leg like a old man in need of his cane. But he wasn't coming out of the lineup.

"You know, we look at Bryant Winslow playing first base with a broken leg, we figure, 'Hey, we might as well go win this thing for him,' " pitcher Pat Cedeno had said earlier in the week.

This was more than a mere broken leg. The bunt that Texas' Lance Jones put down was a good one, so good that Shocker third baseman Mike Jones had to barehand it and make an off-balance throw. Too off-balance, so much so that Winslow had to reach up the line to snare it.

But also up the line was Lance Jones, who plowed into Winslow. As they fell, Winslow's right leg was still anchored on the bag, though

the shin and knee were in grotesquely awkward positions. The scream from Winslow's open mouth said it all.

Doctors and trainers and Gene Stephenson gathered around Winslow, looking at his right leg. He had to come out, but he refused. "I told (Stephenson) I wanted to stay in. So we made a deal. He let me stay in if I stayed off the bag, and we'd see how it went."

But Winslow looked helpless while walking around. "He obviously could not continue," Stephenson said. "I wanted him to come out. Tears were streaming down his face. He didn't want to come out."

So Winslow took his position holding Jones at first as Brummett delivered a pitch. As he pushed off the bag, though, an unforgiving pain shot through Winslow's leg. He asked for time and began hobbling for the dugout before a standing ovation.

"I wasn't into playing macho-man

ing the team after injuring another bone in his right leg, Winslow hobbled off the field in an emotional Rosenblatt moment after trying to stay in for one pitch.

The Shockers, ahead only 3-2 at the time, needed a lift and Meares was there to deliver. With one out, Joey Wilson (Winslow's replacement) singled to center. As he took off on a hit-and-run four pitches later, Meares caught a 2-2 pitch and launched it over the left-field fence for a two-run homer and 5-2 lead.

"Meares' home run was a tremendous lift because there's a lot of difference between a one-run game and a three-run game," Wedge said. "It brought the momentum back our way."

DOWN THE STRETCH WSU wouldn't score again, but did it matter? You just had the feeling that day that three runs in Brummett's hands were going to be enough.

stuff with the national championship on the line," he said. As he passed the pitcher's mound, where Wedge and Brummett had gathered, Winslow looked at Brummett and said, "Don't you dare lose this game."

"Personally, it was hard for us to control our emotions," Wedge said.

Winslow was allowed to stay in the dugout for the remainder of the game, then hobbled out to the field after the game to celebrate. When he received his plaque, he raised his crutch and smiled.

Message delivered.

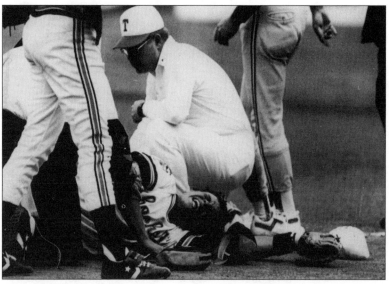

Bryant Winslow's fight to stay in the game summed up the 1989 Shockers' spirit.

Greg Brummett gives President Bush a Shocker jersey during the White House ceremony.

Texas got a run in the sixth on a fielder's choice, but Brummett was unrelenting from there. Over his last three innings, he gave up exactly one walk and no Longhorn reached base in the eighth and ninth. Brummett got the ball back from Wedge, got a sign and worked quickly.

"The great ones always smell the end," Kemnitz said.

When pinch-hitter Kevin Pate struck out in the ninth, Brummett lost it. He jumped up, fell to the ground and finally jumped into Wedge's arms. Spike had spiked Texas, and WSU was No. 1.

"There's not a team that works harder or a team with more heart," Wedge said afterward. "It's just incredible."

MIKE AT THE MIKE The university has had its share of colorful and eloquent radio broadcasters over the years. Rick Weaver, Gus Grebe and Ken Softley were all solid play-by-play men.

Though small today, the opening-day attendance of 1,925 in 1990 was a WSU record.

But none of them brought it from the heart like Mike Kennedy. A Wichita State graduate, Kennedy began his broadcasting career by calling games for campus station KMUW. When Kennedy took the play-by-play job at KAKE radio in the mid-'70s, he was in his own element.

A tireless historian of WSU athletics, Kennedy brings a depth of knowledge of Shocker sports that no one can equal, and his attention to detail in game preparation is hardly ever matched. His six Kansas Sportscaster of the Year awards attest to that.

So when Kennedy called the final game in the 1989 CWS, it had to come with a sense of satisfaction. He had been there for The Battle of New Orleans, for WSU's football win over Kansas in 1982, and for so many other moments in Shocker history. He was inducted into the Shocker Hall of Fame in 1995.

A GREEN GEM There was just one little show of emotion as Tyler Green completed WSU's first nine-inning no-hitter, beating New Mexico 12-0. He raised his first slightly after striking out his 13th Lobo, then had to be picked up by catcher Mike Jones.

"That's just the way I am," Green said. "I'm excited, honest. But being a pitcher, you always have to keep your composure on the mound."

Tyler Green's knuckle-curve was a nasty pitch to hitters.

GOOD DECISION P.J. Forbes wasn't an imposing physical specimen. A small, frail-looking second baseman, he was set to play at a junior college before Wichita State decided that physical stature alone didn't make up this guy.

By the times Forbes left WSU in 1990, he was one of the Shockers' all-time best defensive players. His .985 fielding percentage for a season is the best of any WSU

second baseman.

One of his greatest plays came in the '89 CWS. In the second Florida State game, he went deep behind second base, slid and stabbed a ground ball. He got to his feet and fired a strike to first for the out.

P.J. Forbes' artistry at second base overshadowed a dependable bat.

HOME IS WHERE THE REGIONAL IS "Dear Shocker Fan," the letter began. "I'm going to get an NCAA Baseball Tournament or die trying."

One of Tom Shupe's biggest goals as athletic director was to bring a regional home to Eck Stadium. After two tries himself and five by the university, WSU had met enough of the NCAA's criteria for hosting and was awarded the Midwest Regional.

But by the time WSU learned it would be home for a regional, it was hitting a downward spiral. The Shockers lost two straight home games in the conference tournament, then lost to Georgia Southern and UCLA in the Midwest Regional after disposing of Arkansas.

BACK TO NORMAN? The mood turned from disappointment to outright fright over the next few days after the regional defeat. It became known that the University of Oklahoma was talking with Stephenson about its head coaching job. OU athletic director Donnie Duncan watched the end of the regional, then he and Stephenson met briefly.

Stephenson had come to WSU from Norman after working under Enos Semore, who had retired in January

Gene Stephenson and AD Tom Shupe after Stephenson announced he was staying in Wichita.

1990. His stance was that he was happy at WSU but did not want to shut off other opportunities.

Some fans and boosters went so far as to cut TV commercials urging Stephenson to stay by starting a letter-writing campaign.

BACK TOWARD THE TOP

Stephenson didn't go anywhere, saying "we" had built something from nothing and it was proper to continue the tradition that had been started at Wichita State.

It was the start of a great three-year run for the Shockers. From 1991 to 1993, they made the College World Series each time, twice making it to the national championship game.

The 1991 Shockers were 40-2 at home, a school-best .952 percentage.

"We decided to stay and continue the tradition here because of the people," Stephenson said. "That has to do with the people of Wichita, it has to do with the people at Wichita State University, and it has to do with the players in the program and my coaching staff and all of the people affiliated with Wichita State."

Amazingly, Creighton was picked over WSU as the 1990 Valley favorite.

STEAMROLLING STEENSTRA The finesse that Kennie Steenstra exhibited on the mound fit in perfectly with his personality. Always calm, never ego-driven, Steenstra was a model of consistency for the Shockers.

"He's a guy with three pitches that he can throw for strikes, he puts the ball where he wants it, and he never talks about what he does," teammate Darren Dreifort said.

To Steenstra, winning 17 straight games in 1991 was no big deal. In a game dominated by aluminum bats and high-scoring games, Steenstra's statistics stood out like no others in NCAA history: a 17-0 record with a 2.17

Kennie Steenstra matched his record-setting high school numbers in college.

ERA in 19 starts. No wonder he was a first-team All-America selection.

Then again, winning was nothing new to Steenstra. As a high school student, he pitched Plato High in Lynchburg, Mo., to 65 victories over four years – the most by any prep pitcher in the nation.

BYE-BYE BILLY Reading over Billy Hall's career stats heading into his senior year at WSU wasn't tough. Eleven at-bats, two hits, one stolen base in one season after junior college. This was the Shockers' second baseman for 1991?

"I could tell you stories about people who said he couldn't play," Stephenson said. "That he'd never be a player here."

It sure looked that way, until Hall became an every-day player and blossomed at the top of the lineup. Hitting .364, Hall led the nation in stolen bases with 59 and he, along with Chris Wimmer (54 swipes), was a threat to go every time he got on base.

"I like to get on base and have the pitcher thinking

about me constantly," said Hall, a Wichita native. "He's always thinking, 'Is he going to run? Is he going to run? When is he going to run? I've got to get the ball to the catcher faster.' "

MMM, TASTY On a team with several star players, freshman Jaime Bluma was allowed to blend into the mix without much fanfare. … until he licked a bug off the team bus for $50.

Bug-eating became a national symbol for Bluma, a terrific relief pitcher with a terrific knack for the zany. It was more than bugs. He'd warm up in the bullpen wearing his cap backward and with the string in his pants hanging out.

"When I was young and acting crazy, we had so many stars on the team and so many upperclassmen that I wasn't there to be a leader," Bluma said. "I could just do my own thing."

That thing was throw a moving fastball and a nasty slider to hitters late in games, which usually sealed up a Shocker victory. His 1.60 ERA as a freshman proved he was something special, and after the season he was named one of the nation's 10 best relievers by Baseball America.

SUPER DOWN THE STRETCH Seemingly as usual, WSU found itself out of first place when the Shockers met Creighton in a conference series at Eck. But Wichita State pounded out four wins by a combined score of 43-13 and took over first place, improved its record to 47-10 and took over the top spot in the polls.

The rest of the Valley was a cakewalk. WSU won six more in a row, then allowed only three runs in three conference tournament games to cruise into its Midwest Regional at home.

The Shockers did it the right way in the Midwest Regional this time, failing to lose a game out of four on their own field. WSU knocked off East Carolina, Baylor and California before the Bears rebounded to get back to the championship game.

But WSU's eight-run eighth inning broke open a close game and WSU won 11-5, heading to the CWS for the third time in four years.

'THE GAME OF THEIR LIVES' There have been so many "big" games in Shocker history. But will any be remembered more for the pure emotion and gut-wrenching twists than the first WSU-Creighton game in the '91 CWS?

WSU had won nine straight against Creighton, but that didn't mean much in this game. After all, the Bluejays and Omaha were pumped because the hometown team was playing in the tournament for the first time.

Billy Hall was a full-time player only one season, but led the nation in stolen bases.

Catcher Doug Mirabelli gunned down 46 percent of would-be base stealers in his career.

So when a record crowd of 18,206 filled Rosenblatt Stadium that Monday night, it was one of the few times the majority weren't pulling for WSU. They saw Tyler Green baffle Creighton for nine innings, allowing only two unearned runs in the first and striking out 14.

WSU didn't have much more success off Bluejays starter Alan Benes, scoring two unearned runs in the fourth themselves.

So, inning after inning, batter after batter, pitch after pitch, the intensity in Rosenblatt became electric.

But in the 12th, after Jaime Bluma's wicked slider had set down Creighton for two clean innings, WSU got a break. Jim Audley beat out an infield hit, went to second on a hit-and-run groundout, then to third when Todd Dreifort was intentionally walked but was forced out at second on Mike Jones' grounder.

Scot McCloughan hit a bouncer up the middle that shortstop Bobby Langer had a chance at, but he collided with second baseman Kimera Bartee and Audley scored. It was up to Bluma to take the Shockers home, but he promptly hit Jason Judge to start the inning.

Langer hit a grounder to the hole in right field, but Hall ran it down and threw to first for the out. So with one out, pinch-runner Steve Bruns was at second base.

Dax Jones hit a looper into center field for a hit and Bruns rounded third for the plate. Audley, who had great

Reliever Jaime Bluma was a dependable closer for four years.

Jim Audley got a ride to the dugout after his 12th-inning throw to the plate.

speed but was playing deep, pounced on the ball after one hop and quickly made the throw home.

"As soon as he let go of it, I knew it was going to be right there," Doug Mirabelli said. "It just bounced right up to me. Couldn't have asked for a better throw."

Mirabelli did his part, too. He stood like a statue at the plate, hoping Bruns would think the throw was being cut off. But it wasn't. Mirabelli took the one-hop throw in his glove, lowered his body, cut off the plate with his left knee and made the tag.

Out. A grounder to short then turned off Rosenblatt's emotion meter.

"We were beyond being excited," Audley said the next day. "It's almost like being nervous. You can't believe you do what you just did."

To this day, you can occasionally see highlights of the game packaged into a half-hour show on ESPN. They know classics when they see them.

Todd Dreifort (above) homered and Darren Dreifort (below) pitched as WSU won the 1992 regional at Eck.

GOOD FORTUNE GOES SOUTH WSU disposed of Creighton again two days later 11-3, meaning a second championship-game appearance in three years.

The opponent was Louisiana State, and the Tigers jumped on Green, who wasn't as sharp as in his Creighton start. He gave up four runs in two innings, and the Shockers couldn't come back with only five hits off LSU pitching.

"We've come out flat against a lot of teams, but our talent's been able to overcome the people we've been playing," Todd Dreifort said. "Today, it just seemed like we came out flat and stayed flat."

So WSU, which went 50-6 after a 16-7 start, wasn't at its best on the biggest day of the season. But Stephenson looked at the big picture instead of the wallet size.

"We far exceeded anything that anyone on the outside of our program believed was possible this year," Stephenson said. "Everything we did was excellent for building toward this national championship game. We've got nothing to be disappointed about."

HOG-WHOMPED Steenstra came back for his senior season just as sharp as in 1991, winning his first eight decisions and coming within one victory of tying the NCAA record for consecutive winning decisions.

But the Shockers, ranked No. 1 with a 29-1 record, found it tough going against Arkansas. The Razorbacks got five runs off Steenstra in seven innings, and while that would be OK some nights, the Shockers' bats didn't come through and the streak was over one game shy of the record set by BYU's Scott Nielsen.

In typical Steenstra humility, he said, "This sort of thing happens. I didn't pitch as well as I wanted to." The loss also broke WSU's 41-game home winning streak.

Steenstra would still have a great season, going 13-2. But somehow, a first-team All-American was overlooked for even first- or second-team All-Valley honors his final season.

MOTHER OF ALL SLUMPS First it was 3 of 4. Then 4 of 6, finally 6 of 8. The Shockers were playing bad baseball; Stephenson called it a "grand funk."

The losses were to quality competition – Arkansas, Creighton, Oklahoma and Oklahoma State among them – but Stephenson wouldn't accept losses to the '27 Yankees, either.

"I've been involved in college coaching for close to 25 years," he said after a 3-2 loss at Kansas State. "I've never had a team that cannot or will not respond to adversity. There are just a lot of questions in my mind right now."

Shortstop Chris Wimmer was a two-year member of Team USA.

CAN-DO CHARLIE Charlie Giaudrone was never THE guy in the Shocker pitching staff. First there was Greg Brummett, then Kennie Steenstra, then Darren Dreifort. Never was Giaudrone the guy better than everybody else.

But if the Shockers ever needed a big-game performance, Giaudrone was there. He won the '89 regional-clinching game against Michigan and a big CWS game against Florida State, and his four-year numbers – 31-7 record, 2.69 ERA – prove he was one of WSU's all-time best.

From McAlester, Okla., Giaudrone was also one of the smartest players to ever wear a Shocker uniform. A two-time Academic All-American, Giaudrone in 1992 was named the national Academic Athlete of the Year by the nation's sports information directors.

Charlie Giaudrone came up big in crucial games.

QUICK TRIP Of WSU's six trips to the College World Series, four have gone to the final day and another was a game short of that.

Then there was 1992, when the Shockers were tamed by Orel Hershiser and boarded the bus home two days later. In a nationally televised opener, Patrick Ahearne of Pepperdine – who patterned his entire pitching philosophy around Hershiser, the then-Dodgers star – three-hit WSU in a 6-0 win. In the loser's bracket, Oklahoma jumped on Darren Dreifort in the sixth inning for four hits and five runs in two-thirds of an inning. WSU lost 8-4.

"It sucks to come out and not have your best stuff," Dreifort said. "This is the College World Series. How can you be good all year and not pitch a good game here?"

A NEW-FANGLED STADIUM You know you've hit the big-time when it's so cold to warm up, a relief pitcher enters the game off of an elevator.

That's exactly what Dreifort did in the 1993 opener, though. While warming up in the third-floor bullpen of Eck Stadium's new clubhouse facility, Dreifort was called in to face an Illinois-Chicago hitter. So he hopped on the elevator and got a key strikeout.

"I was changing my spikes in the elevator on the way down," Dreifort said later.

WRECKING TECH One of the strangest plays of the Shocker season was against Georgia Tech in the Atlantic Regional's second round. Committing two errors that led to a Tech run in the top of the 10th, WSU was one out away from the loss when Toby Smith singled to left with two men on.

Hall scored easily, but the Yellow Jackets' third baseman threw home anyway. The ball got away from catcher Jason Varitek, and Richie Taylor rounded third and headed home with the winning run.

After an afternoon loss temporarily knocked the Shockers off course, they beat Ohio State in the nightcap to earn their fifth CWS appearance in six years. It also meant that nine freshman classes, dating back to 1985, had an opportunity to play in Omaha in June.

DINK THOSE HORNS Two days after an 11-inning victory over Arizona State, WSU met Texas in the CWS' second round. And this one topped the Georgia Tech victory in terms of wackiness.

The eighth-inning rally that got the Shockers past Texas 7-6 consisted of four runs and only one ball hit out of the infield: infield single, walk, walk, RBI walk, two-run single to right, walk and finally a one-run error by the Texas shortstop.

"I still say the same thing I've been saying," Stephenson said. "You don't ever want to leave a game we're involved in because anything is liable to happen, whether we're way ahead or way behind."

WSU handled rival Oklahoma State 10-4 in the bracket final, putting the Shocks in the national championship game for the third time in five years. The opponent was LSU, again.

NOT THEIR DAY In batting practice before the national championship game, Dreifort and other Shockers were hitting balls out of the park with ease. Stephenson fidgeted behind the cage.

"Anytime we take batting practice and hit a lot of fly balls and home runs, I'm worried," he would say later. "We like our hitters to hit on top of the ball, and if they're hitting under it in batting practice, they usually hit even more under it during the game."

22. What pitcher holds the WSU single-game strikeout record?

Center fielder Richie Taylor hit .385 in his fourth year as a starter.

23. Excluding the 1993 expansion teams, how many major-league clubs have never signed a Shocker?

Only in this game, LSU starter Brett Laxton made sure the Shockers didn't make contact at all. He struck out 16 WSU batters, a CWS record, as the Tigers won easily 8-0.

"He came at us with his fastball all day and pretty much stuck it in our … " Dreifort said, finishing the sentence with a body part. "There's really nothing else you can say about it."

So on a day when the Shockers had hoped to finish a magical season with the ultimate prize, there instead was a somber mood with the realization that they hadn't been at their best in the big game.

"The unfortunate thing is that the only thing anybody

24. Who's the only Shocker to have a flawless fielding season?

GOLDEN RELIEVER

Before and during the 1993 season, Darren Dreifort was being touted as the probable No. 1 pick in the June amateur draft, which would make him the highest drafted Shocker since Joe Carter 12 years earlier. That would command a signing bonus of maybe $2 million.

Scouts drooled over Darren Dreifort's pitching ability.

It was enough to make most players' heads spin. But not Dreifort. Accompanying his blazing fastball and nasty slider was enough common sense to let him know that there are no guarantees in life.

So Dreifort stayed focus, remaining Wichita State's prize middle reliever. Pitching a little more than three innings per appearance, Dreifort earned an 11-1 record with four saves, a 2.48 ERA and a phenomenal 1.3-strike-outs-per-inning-ratio.

His collegiate honors were endless: 1992 Olympian, two-time All-America, and the winner of two Player of the Year awards: the 1993 R.E. "Bob" Smith and Golden Spikes awards.

When draft time came, he was No. 2 and chosen by the Dodgers. The signing bonus was $1.3 million, at that time the second-largest bonus in history. But, as always, Dreifort wasn't shaken by the figures.

"I drive a 1985 Dodge Colt with about 78,000 miles on it," he said. "I really don't own much, but that's OK. I have my family and I have my health."

Brent Kemnitz has coached five conference Pitchers of the Year.

Shane Dennis' struggling junior season was followed by a 9-2, 1.35 ERA senior year.

ever remembers is the champion," Stephenson said. "It's unfortunate that they're only going to remember the last game. It was almost a Cinderella story. Almost. We almost pulled it off."

'I DESPISE HITTERS' Dreifort earned All-America honors in 1993, becoming another feather in the highly decorated cap of Shocker pitching coach Brent Kemnitz. Also in charge of recruiting and scheduling for the Shockers, Kemnitz has a long list of accomplishments by his pitchers:

One NCAA Player of the Year, 13 All-America pitchers, 45 All-Missouri Valley pitchers and two staffs that led the nation in ERA ('82, '91).

"As a pitcher, you've got to go out and command a game, because the instant a hitter starts getting to you ... " Kemnitz said. "That works a nerve with me so unbelievably that I can't even describe it."

Kemnitz pitched at Phillips University, where he was 21-7 in his career, including an 8-0 junior season.

HALL MONITOR As WSU rolled to the 1994 Valley title with a 19-2 record, Carl Hall was heating up. He batted .354 his senior season, 18 points higher than any of his three previous years as a starter.

More than that, though, Hall was healthy and consistent again. A back injury that made him miss the 1991 season was gone, and Hall was in the midst of a stretch of hitting over .400 when postseason play came around.

But Illinois State and Bradley bit the host Shocks in the Valley Tournament, meaning WSU wouldn't be the No. 1 seed for its own Midwest Regional.

Instead, Georgia Tech came in as the team to beat. WSU couldn't touch the Yellow Jackets after a 2-1 first-round loss to Santa Clara, a game in which Dennis allowed only two runs but couldn't get offensive help. The next day, the Yellow Jackets repaid WSU for winning the '93 regional at Atlanta, pounding the Shocks 13-1.

FINALLY, A RUN Through 10 games and 18 1/3 innings of NCAA Tournament action, Bluma had been perfect. No runs given up.

But that finally ended in his senior season,

and in a meaningless fashion. Mopping up in the Shockers' 13-1 loss to Georgia Tech, Bluma worked a third of an inning and gave up a hit and a run.

Certainly not the end of the world. Barely a year after his collegiate career ended, Bluma was at Kansas City's Triple-A club in Omaha. His climb of four pro levels in that time included four months as a Wichita Wrangler, where he tied the club record for saves (22).

A BRIGHT FUTURE Despite winning Stephenson's 1,000th game at WSU, the 1995 Shockers didn't make the College World Series, which these days meant an off year. Expectations have become so high for the program that people scratch their heads when WSU loses a game anytime, be it February or June.

But there are signs that the Shockers will be strong for years to come. First baseman-pitcher Ben Thomas certainly has the potential to be as devastating a two-way player as Darren Dreifort. Casey Blake and Braden Looper were members of the U.S. National team. The pitching staff is young and deep, too, with three full-time starters and the three top relievers all returning.

That's just the near future. As for long-term, just take a look at Eck Stadium – the majestic grandstands, the country club-like facilities, the larger-than-life scoreboard – and know that there's really no down baseball year at WSU.

The man had a heck of a vision, didn't he?

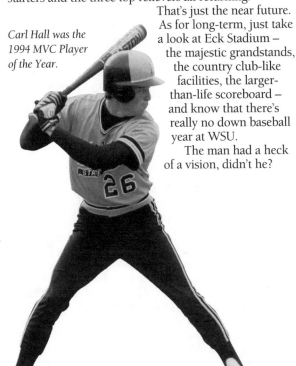

Carl Hall was the 1994 MVC Player of the Year.

Jason Adams (above) and Joey Jackson (below) were stellar in the middle infield.

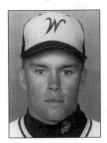

Mike Drumright was a first-round draft pick after his 11-3 junior season.

Football

For many, thoughts of football at Wichita State understandably start with tragedy and sorrow. Some say the beginning to the end of the football program after the 1986 season was Oct. 2, 1970, the day that 31 Shocker players, coaches and boosters died in a plane crash on Mount Trelease in Colorado.

WSU had just two winning seasons after the 1970 crash, while community apathy, financial problems and empty Cessna Stadium seats increased. Finally, on Dec. 2, 1986, university President Warren Armstrong announced the end of football at WSU, saying, "I must do what my head knows is right in meeting any fiduciary responsibilities even though my heart is not in it."

But that's where Shocker football ends. What many people don't remember – or choose to remember – are the beginnings.

Long forgotten are the contributions that early Fairmount College teams made to the evolution of college football, or the standout teams coached by Al Gebert in the 1930s. Or the three bowl appearances and some pretty good squads in the early 1960s.

Wichita State's overall football record was 375-402-47, a winning percentage of .482. Not earth-shattering, but not horrible, either. If Shocker football should ever make a return, remember more than the negatives. Remember Linwood Sexton, Jimmy Nutter and Prince McJunkins, among others. Remember Saturday afternoons at the stadium when the Shockers may not have won, but at least they were fun to watch.

QUIZ

25. What was Theodore Morrison's faculty position at Fairmount College?

A FAIRMOUNT FOLLY

In 1896, college football was steadily gaining popularity throughout the United States. In Wichita, The Sunday Daily Eagle would usually carry an account of the previous day's big Ivy League game on the front page.

Around town, football moved much more slowly. Friends University formed a team, as did Wichita High School. Male students at Fairmount also worked at forming a squad but couldn't come up with enough players. So that fall, a team of Fairmount students and some other townspeople took on Wichita High School, though it isn't regarded as WSU's first football game. Faculty members such as Theodore H. Morrison, who would later coach the team, played in the game.

The High School won, though the loss didn't detract from a spirit that saw fans excited about the prospects of

The 1897 Fairmount College football team, the school's first squad, which won its only game, 12-4 over Wichita High School.

being able to watch their school play a game. Noted the Sunflower: "Foot-ball has already become established in Fairmount, but for some reason the proper spirit seems to be lacking. … Boys, be loyal to your college; don your canvas suits and work. The foot-ball record of Fairmount is at stake."

FAIRMOUNT'S OWN The men on the hill had better luck in 1897. With a full squad assembled, Fairmount scheduled its one-and-only game, again with Wichita High School. The Daily Eagle's account on Nov. 20, 1897:

COLLEGE BOYS WIN

Fairmount Wins Against High School by Score of 12 to 4

"The long-advertised football contest between Fairmount College and the Wichita High School teams was played yesterday afternoon on the Garfield Gridiron. The game was a rouse from start to finish. The interest and enthusiasm on the part of the friends of the respective teams was at fever heat through the entire game."

Against a smaller high school team, Fairmount took a 2-0 lead on a safety and scored a touchdown (worth four points) for a 6-0 halftime lead. Wichita High scored a "controversial" touchdown with an alleged forward lateral to trail 6-4, then Fairmount scored again to pull away. The Eagle summed up Fairmount's first game in a positive tone:

"It is a matter of congratulations to both teams that a clean game as played throughout. There was no slugging or unnecessary roughness. It was clean, manly sport. Both teams played with courage, skill, pluck and coolness.… While both teams played well, the Fairmount team won on superior skill and knowledge of the game."

Played today, this game would be looked at strangely, a college team beating up on a high school bunch. But not in 1897. Fairmount was tickled to win its first game. Morrison, who had come to Wichita to practice law after graduating from Northwestern Law School, gave an impassioned, 700-word plea in the Sunflower following the victory. He appealed for school support, financing, more players, an athletic field and, most of all, a punter. "A drop-kicker we can do without," he wrote, "but a punter we must have."

CAN'T WIN 'EM ALL By the fall of 1898, football at Fairmount was still not a weekly occurrence, though the hill men

FAIRMOUNT'S PLACE IN COLLEGI

In the span of three months in 1905, Fairmount College was responsible for more college football innovations than other schools can dream of. Next time you watch a college game, imagine no forward passes or no night games. Then think back to 1905 and a couple of games at Wichita's Association Park.

The first milestone came on Oct. 6, when Fairmount met Cooper College (now Sterling) in the second game of the season. Roy Kirk, the innovative student manager for the Fairmount team, arranged to have 30 gas lights hung from poles on both sides and at the ends of the Association Park field and the nation's first night college football game west of the Missouri River was played.

A rousing success? Well, sort of. The sides of the field were well-lit, but the center needed more light. Also, whenever a team punted, the ball (painted white for easier visibil-ity) went above the lights and was hard to spot by the return man.

But the experiment served its purpose. Fairmount enjoyed better attendance with the night game, and fans were generally enthused with the lighting. Fairmount won 24-0.

That wasn't all in '05, though. By then, college football was entering a dangerous time in its brief history. Without the padding and protection of today's game, the season became one of the worst player fatality-ridden seasons in football history. Players were suffering broken bones and other injuries at an alarming rate.

President Theodore Roosevelt called for reform of the game, and Fairmount College was there to help. With Roosevelt's blessing, Fairmount met Washburn University in a Christmas Day postseason game played at Wichita's Association Park under a special set of rules.

gave it the ol' college try. In October, the squad announced the cancellation of its games because Athletic Park, the scheduled site for the contests, had to be torn down. But Fairmount was able to schedule one game, against natural cross-town rival Friends on Nov. 19. It would be Fairmount's first game against a college opponent.

Friends was already 0-1-1 after a scoreless tie with Wichita High and a 10-0 loss to a team from Newton. The Daily Eagle told readers that "Everybody should remember the date of the game and be present at this exciting contest. There will be special street car service."

Fairmount lost 5-0, never generating any offense. Injuries to a pair of key players didn't help. The only score came about eight minutes in, when Friends halfback Baldwin went through the line for a touchdown. But according to the Daily Eagle, there was as much excitement off the field as on:

"From across the river came a goodly crowd of

Of WSU's 375 football wins, 40 percent came by shutout (150).

FOOTBALL HISTORY

In the experimental game, the offense needed 10 yards in three downs for a first down instead of only 5 yards. This change, suggested by Yale coach Walter Camp, was made to open up the game. Conventional offenses were used to sending a back up the middle since only 5 yards were needed for a first down. As The Eagle noted in previewing the game, "This will practically compel the abolition of the mass play, making the game more open and thus removing one of the most serious objections to the sport."

There were other changes for this special game: The forward pass was allowed if thrown behind the line of scrimmage; a field goal was worth more points if kicked from farther back on the field; a player cited for slugging an opponent was disqualified and the team either lost the ball (if on offense) or was penalized 25 yards (if on defense); and a

team was penalized 15 yards for piling on the man with the ball.

Understandably, the new rules made for an uncertain game. Neither team got close to scoring, as both had a hard time figuring out how to get first downs. There were only seven in the game, with a total of 38 punts. But the new rules certainly cut down injuries, as no player left the game because of roughness.

But more important than the first-down rule was a different kind of milestone. In the first half, Fairmount back Ben Davis threw a primitive, two-handed toss to end Art Solter that went for 10 yards and is believed to be the first forward pass in college football history. Fans were delighted at the passing they saw, according to The Eagle: "The fact that that the ball was in the air a good deal also pleased the populace, who evidently delighted in seeing the egg-shaped ball float across the horizon."

*In the December
1900 Sunflower, a
parody of what foot-
ball rules should read
had these two notes:
1. No one is to inten-
tionally kill a player
already wounded.
2. Killed or wounded
must leave the field
at once.*

Quaker maidens wearing the scarlet and gray of their heroes, while the Fairmount maidens simply turned out en mass, all bedecked with the yellow that their idols were defending. It is unnecessary to say that the two delegations did not mix."

"A young lady at the Fairmount game said she knew (Fairmount) would get beat as one of their players did not have long hair, but was getting bald."

A RECURRING THEME

After two games in two years, Fairmount became serious about playing a full schedule. The hill men (as they were often referred to because of the college's location northeast of Wichita) played five games in 1899, though none were against other colleges. But in the first three seasons under Coach Harry Hess, a star player at Kansas before graduating and coming to Fairmount, Fairmount won 10, lost 10 and tied twice.

WE'RE THE BEST By the end of the 1899 season, Fairmount supporters were getting quite used to football – and winning. Even though Fairmount was only 2-1-2 in 1899, the Sunflower wrote, "We can hardly lay claim to the championship of southwestern Kansas, but we are safe in saying that our team is a peer to any in this section."

That came days after Fairmount's second win of the season, a 7-0 shutout of Wichita High School. The High School was a late replacement for Winfield's town team, which telegraphed that it could not make the trip. The High School gathered its players with three hours' notice.

Willis Bates was the most successful coach of any to last more than one season, winning 78.7 percent of his games.

A NEW CENTURY STARTS RIGHT The Fairmount team of 1900 was 5-3, which was cause for celebration around campus. Professor C.C. Isely, president of the school's athletic association, brought the players to his home for a postseason dinner of royal oyster stew. The Sunflower reported, "The lustiness of the College yell, given as the guests departed, was a harbinger of success for next year's conflicts."

A DOMINATING DECADE Almost immediately after starting a full schedule of football, Fairmount College became an imposing opponent for Midwestern teams in the 1900s. Over a seven-year period, beginning in 1902, Fairmount reeled off seven consecutive winning seasons, compiling a 41-17-4 record. Never again would a Wichita State team match that string. More impressively, though, were the 33 shutouts Fairmount recorded.

One of those shutouts came against Christian College of Enid, Okla., on Nov. 11, 1907. Against an Enid team that was playing its first season, Fairmount won 111-0,

scoring 87 first-half points. The Eagle summarized: "At any time when they felt so disposed, they would force one of the their heavy men through the line for a touch-down or a long run."

FAIR-WEATHER FANS On Nov. 23, 1905, Fairmount beat Winfield's town team 11-0; continual storms, mud and wind wreaked havoc on the two teams. The reported attendance: Eight men and a boy. Gate receipts: $2.20.

THE NOT-SO-ROARING '20s Football went quietly from the

The 1908 Fairmount team went 8-1 and outscored opponents 256-32.

The 1911 Wheatshockers won the Kansas Conference championship.

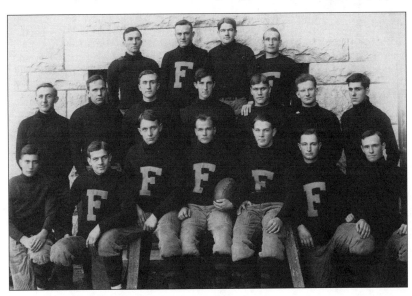

Fairmount College era into the University of Wichita era. There were some good teams in that time – seven winning seasons from 1909 to 1929 – but none enjoyed as much success as the teams of the 1930s.

That's when Al Gebert came to town.

THE NOTRE DAME WAY

Knute Rockne recommended Al Gebert to WU boosters.

In the spring of 1930, WU supporter Jess Harper knew what his school needed in a football coach. After all, Harper had coached Notre Dame in the mid-1910s and one of his pupils was Knute Rockne. Harper called Rockne, by then the Fighting Irish's legendary coach, and asked for a recommendation.

Al Gebert hit the road for Kansas.

Gebert wasn't a star player for Rockne at Notre Dame. He wasn't even a starter. He was only a backup quarterback. But Gebert had a great mind for the game, and standing on the same sideline with Rockne helped him learn even more.

After graduation from South Bend, WU officials hired Gebert, 23, immediately on Rockne's approval.

Gebert would bring something that the university would never really have again: stability in a head football coach. Gebert was in charge for 12 years, coached 10 winning seasons and brought consistency to WU football.

Al Gebert installed the Notre Dame system at WU and enjoyed 12 years of success.

OFF TO A GOOD START Gebert wasn't initially worried about his team's physical condition or abilities, but he was worried that his Shockers weren't grasping his Notre Dame-dominated style. So Gebert closed his practices to fans and the press, making sure there were no distractions.

Just about everybody thought WU would be a big underdog in its opener against Oklahoma A&M at Stillwater on Sept. 26, 1930. The Aggies were bigger and more experienced, but Gebert's system worked and WU hung tough. A&M won 12-0, but the WU coaching staff attributed the scoring margin to depth. A&M used 40 players, Wichita only 14.

Putting Al Gebert's years in perspective

Tenure (12 years): Seven years more than any other coach

Wins (68): Forty more than any other coach

TAKE THAT, TURKEY A nice tradition began in the early days of football at WU. On Thanksgiving Day, the Shockers would meet cross-town rival Friends. Gebert stressed the game to his players in 1930 and they responded, pummeling the Quakers 33-0 and outgaining them 394 yards to 36.

THE GEBERT GENIUS Wichita was 6-3-1 in Gebert's first season, then 15-5 over the next two with the university's first two Central Conference championships.

Clearly, Gebert was taking Wichita to a new level of

college football.

The Eagle chronicled Gebert's winning ways: "Kicked about over the conference for years, the Shockers stand today as the greatest team within the realms of the Central Conference and one which is feared throughout the country."

"I was smarter than all the rest of the coaches in this area," Gebert told The Wichita Eagle-Beacon 50 years after his arrival. "I knew more about football than the rest of the guys who were coaching those days. I'd had better training and in a system that was completely foreign to them. And I used everything I learned at Notre Dame."

Gebert coached nine more years at WU, gaining four more conference crowns and seven more winning seasons. WU dominated the Central Conference so much that by 1940 it left the league after winning three straight titles.

Frankly, the Shockers were looking for more competition.

University president W.M. Jardine recommended Gebert not be rehired.

ALL GOOD THINGS ... By 1941, maybe the Shockers had found that competition they were looking for. That, and Wichita didn't have the same strengths as previous seasons. Whatever the reason, WU finished with a 1-6-1 record, losing or tying four teams it had beaten the year before.

At the end of the season, university president W.M. Jardine recommended to the school's Board of Regents that Gebert's contract not be renewed. The regents agreed and Gebert was gone. The reason given was not a

A Wichita fullback gains yardage in the Shockers' 33-0 victory over Kansas State Teachers College (Pittsburg) in 1937.

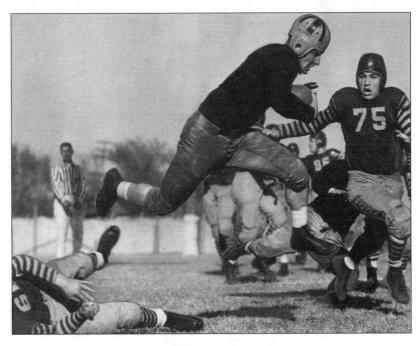

losing season – only the second in Gebert's 12 years – but what the Sunflower reported as "wide differences on athletic policy (that) have existed between Mr. Gebert and the university for some time."

Gebert made it seem as if off-field differences were not the problem, saying: "Before leaving, I would like to extend my thanks to the faculty for its fine cooperation during the past 12 years. An idea was created that feelings between the faculty and myself were not friendly, but I think that the faculty is aware I know this not to be true."

'RAMMING' RALPH The man brought in to rework the power that Gebert formed was familiar to WU fans only because he was once a Shocker killer.

In 1931, a year that Wichita tied for the Central Conference championship, the Shockers lost badly to intrastate rival Kansas State 20-6. The star of that Manhattan team was Ralph Graham, a powerful half-back. Noted the Eagle: "When 'Ramming' Ralph Graham was inserted, the Wichita cause was lost. There seemed to be no stopping him – up to that time the teams appeared to be evenly matched."

Graham took over WU in 1942 and coached the Shockers to a 5-4 record that first season, including a 9-0 blanking of his alma mater, K-State.

THE WAR YEARS World War II prevented WU from having a team in 1943, and while Graham was in the Navy, basketball coach Mel Binford coached the Shockers to an 11-6-1 record in 1944 and '45, the year WU joined the Missouri Valley Conference. By 1946, Graham was back to coach one of WU's finest eras.

SHOCKERS GO BOWLING

After returning from the Navy, Ralph Graham led WU to its first-ever bowl game.

Even though the Munies (a sometimes-used nickname for WU teams, short for Municipals) were 5-5 in 1946, they showed signs that big things were on the horizon.

Graham had returned from a naval stint in World War II and brought some talent with him, among them talented end Anton "Hap" Houlik. Art Hodges also returned after service, and along with Linwood Sexton, who had already established himself as the league's premier halfback with two all-conference seasons, and WU was on its way. Hodges led the Valley in rushing and ranked ninth nationally; and Houlik set a school record with a 108-yard kickoff return.

It was coming together.

BRINGING HOME THE BALL Sexton was enjoying another all-conference season in 1946, but because he was black

WHAT'S IN A NAME?

If you're a Shocker fan, you've been through this before.

Maybe you take your long-lost cousin to a basketball game, or you're wearing a WSU T-shirt while on vacation. Either way, somebody unfamiliar with the university sees this gold and black creature with some kind of grass growing on his head.

The question is common: What's a Shocker?

In the early 1900s, when school wasn't in session, the majority of Fairmount football players earned money for college by working in the wheat harvest. It was believed that the grueling work helped the players get ready for 60-minute football battles.

After spring classes ended, the players rode the horse-drawn street car to Union Station, where they waited for farmers to hire them for the harvest season. Most started south of Wichita, working north as the wheat ripened. This was in the days before the combine, when men shocked by hand the bundles that were left by the binder.

That's where the original Fairmount nickname – Wheatshocker – came from.

The inventor of the nickname was the team manager, Roy Kirk. He invented the name "Wheat Shockers" as part of a poster advertising Fairmount's upcoming game with the Chilocco Indians.

Roy Kirk

In big letters, Kirk had put the word INDIANS under the name Chilocco on the poster. A press agent for the Wichita Fall Festival, which was helping promote the game, demanded that a nickname be given the Fairmount team to balance the INDIANS on the poster.

Kirk also worked for the campus newspaper, The Sunflower, and one day was short of copy. Because the football players worked on the wheat harvest in the summer, Kirk believed it would be a good story and used "Wheat Shocker" in the story, and it stuck.

Over the years, the name was gradually shortened to Shockers, to a point where hardly anybody uses Wheatshockers anymore. The Shocker mascot, an animated shock of wheat outfitted in a black sweater, has been deemphasized in recent years, in favor of a logo with the WSU letters interlocked with two stalks of wheat.

Still, WSU has one of the nation's most unique mascots – even if most people don't know what the heck it is.

was not allowed to make the trip to Canyon, Texas, for the West Texas State game.

"They had told me they were going to bring the ball back for me after they won the game," Sexton said. "Well, they didn't win the game, but Ray Scooterbug Morrison took off with the ball."

It wasn't that easy, though. Assistant coach Jim Trimble had been in a jawing match with some West Texas State supporters and was cornered by them, so the players had to return to the field to help their coach.

Buffaloes fans followed the WU bus back to nearby Amarillo, where the team boarded the train to Wichita. West Texas initially refused to pay the guarantee money to WU until the football was returned, but the Shockers never gave it up.

Today, the ball sits in Sexton's home, autographed by his teammates.

Despite opponents' cheap shots – both physical and verbal – Linwood Sexton's high-kneed running style made him WU's premier back of the 1940s.

PRIDE OF McPHERSON While many of WU's standouts of the late 1940s and '50s came from out of state, Jimmy Nutter was a local kid from up the road in McPherson. As the 1947 WU press guide put it: "In the Nutter household in McPherson, Kansas, Jimmy Nutter is one of eight. But in Wichita, he's one in a million."

Maybe the most versatile athlete in Wichita history, Nutter was a four-sport standout (football, basketball, baseball, track), but he probably gained the most noteriety on the football field, where he was part of some of WU's best teams.

Early in the 1947 season, Nutter was at his best. After three games, he led the nation in yards per carry with 16.67.

And he was in his first season. Nutter, who was only 5-foot-9 and 165 pounds, would eventually play in two bowl games, be named All-Valley in 1949 and second team in 1950, earn 14 varsity letters and be named an academic Senior Honor Man.

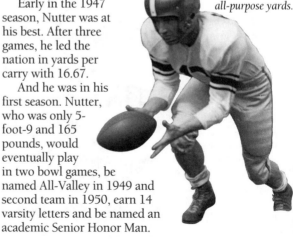

Jimmy Nutter had a school-best 4,469 all-purpose yards.

Anton "Hap" Houlik scored WU's first TD in a 91-0 victory.

THE HATED HURRICANE Wichita and Tulsa played meaningful games long before and long after the 1947 matchup in Tulsa. But there is no more shining example of how a rivalry develops than that weekend.

Both teams were unbeaten in Valley play and it quickly became apparent that the game's winner would have the best chance at the conference title. Neither team

RUNNING OVER RACISM

While his teammates rested comfortably at the swank Sheraton Jefferson Hotel in St. Louis, Linwood Sexton couldn't sleep. The nightclub one floor below his room blasted music all night.

Sexton was black and not allowed, in St. Louis anyway, to stay at the team hotel.

"All of your life, you're conditioned to know that at home you can't eat downtown," Sexton said. "In high school when you went somewhere, you had to stay with a black family, you couldn't stay with the team."

Despite staying by himself and being unable to sleep, Sexton rushed for 175 yards the next day as WU beat St. Louis 13-0 in 1946. As it did his whole career, Sexton's exceptional skill and courage spoke volumes.

College football was no different from the rest of society when it came to racism. Sexton sometimes couldn't stay at the same hotel, eat at the same restaurant, or even play in some road games.

With the Valley title on the line at 1947, Sexton couldn't play in Tulsa. WU lost 7-0. When he did play, Sexton knew he was a target.

"I had decent speed, plus at that time being the only black on the team, you had all kinds of conversations from opposing players," Sexton said. "They called me

everything but a child of God."

Sexton, the Shockers' first three-time All-Missouri Valley selection, finished with 1,995 yards in four years, impressive numbers for that era of football.

Graduating from Wichita East, Sexton had a couple of college options. He could go to a black college in the south, but Sexton had seen enough racism in Wichita to know that he didn't want to try the south.

So it was WU, where he quickly fit in as a student and teammate, not a black student and black teammate.

"I remember sitting on the curb in front of our house when (Melvin Binford) offered me the scholarship," said Sexton, who has remained an active WSU supporter as a member of the Kansas Board of Regents, the WSU Board of Trustees and the Alumni Association board.

"My dad had always said if you are ever going to get anything out of life, you've got to get your education. You're still going to have problems ahead of you, but you'll have your education."

Four years later, immediately after the Raisin Bowl, the Shockers retired the No. 66 of a man who couldn't sit at the Woolworth's counter on Douglas.

In 1947, six Shockers (Linwood Sexton, Art Hodges, Jimmy Nutter, Anton Houlik, Ray Morrison and Eddie Kriwiel) were among the Valley's top 12 in rushing.

could be touched by any other MVC foe.

So Wichita's players and fans looked forward to this one with a fervor not often seen in Shocker football. A caravan of fans headed to T-Town for the game, with Shocker supporters going so far as to hold a parade in downtown Tulsa before kickoff.

In a tight struggle, Tulsa got the only score and won 7-0, eventually winning the conference crown. The Hurricane coaching staff admitted their team had played its very best game to tame the Shockers, who were playing without Sexton. He could not play in Tulsa simply because he was black.

Before the '48 season, the MVC ended all racial discrimination in the conference, partially because of a resolution passed by WSU's Student Council.

CALIFORNIA, HERE WE COME Outscoring opponents 257-89, Wichita earned a bid to the Raisin Bowl on Jan. 1, 1948, in Fresno, Calif. The opponent was the College of the Pacific, led by future NFL quarterback Eddie LeBaron.

About 600 supporters and the WU marching band sent off the Shockers from Union Station on Dec. 28 at 2:05 a.m. Thirty-six hours later, the squad arrived in Fresno for two days of practice.

Graham, who had already announced he was leaving WU after the season to coach at Kansas State, didn't care that his team was a 14-point underdog. "These boys, when they're right," Graham said, "are liable to whip nearly any team."

Most of the players on the 1948 squad played in two bowl games in one calendar year.

BOWL RECORD 0-1 The Shockers beat the spread, but not Pacific. Pacific rushed for almost 400 yards and held WU to under 100 in a 26-14 victory.

Wichita led 7-6 after one quarter but trailed 13-7 by the end of the third. A touchdown by Hodges in the fourth quarter later made it 20-14, but Pacific got a touchdown with under four minutes to play for the final margin.

The season ended there, but changes came quickly. Line coach Jim Trimble was tabbed to take over for Graham; Sexton graduated and played one year for the professional Los Angeles Dons.

26. What movie (and future TV) star dropped by the WU hotel to wish the Shockers luck before the Raisin Bowl?

BOWL RECORD 0-2 A sure sign that Shocker football was receiving national recognition was the 1948 season. Despite a 5-3-1 record and blowout losses to Miami (Ohio) and Nevada, WU was selected to play in the Camilia Bowl on Dec. 30, 1948, in Lafayette, La. Hardin-Simmons was the opponent.

Similar result, though. Hardin-Simmons ran for 314 yards and amassed more than 530 yards in total offense as the Shockers were mowed under 49-12.

CHICAGO-BORN, SHOCKER-BRED One of the mainstays of Wichita's most successful football teams was Eddie Kriwiel, who played in two bowl games and set 17 career school records in his time as a Shocker player.

Kriwiel arrived in Wichita to go to WU and never returned to his hometown of Chicago. Most of his passing records held up for 17 years, before John Eckman's terrific 1966 season. Kriwiel held the career passing yardage record (3,516 yards) until the early 1980s and record for the most touchdown passes (4) until 1977.

After graduation, Kriwiel became the Wichita City League's premier football coach. First at West, then at Kapaun Mount Carmel, Kriwiel won 300 games before retiring in 1991. Sandwiched in there was the 1968 season, when Kriwiel was the Shockers' head coach.

MORE THAN A SHUTOUT Following two consecutive bowl appearances, the 1949 season was regarded as a disappointment. The Shockers scrapped to a 3-6-1 record, though they did beat rival Tulsa 27-21.

There was one other highlight that year, though: a 91-0 trouncing of Northern State Teachers College of Aberdeen, S.D. It wasn't a school record for points or margin of victory (remember the 111-0 win in 1907), but it was a strange day at Veterans Field.

WU put up 14 touchdowns in the game, including 19 points in the first three minutes – all

Eddie Kriwiel held many WU passing records for more than a decade.

In 1950, a "Kitchen Quarterbacks" club met weekly to learn more about WU football. Here, they watch film of the previous week's game.

before the Shocker offense had even stepped on the field. Houlik took the opening kickoff 94 yards, Nutter scored the first of his six touchdowns on an 84-yard punt return, then Eddie Zegler returned an interception 45 yards for another six.

Trimble tried to hold down the score, substituting often and even putting players at new positions. Linebacker J.D. Edminston later recalled that some linemen played fullback.

Northern State coach Clark Swisher had been in Wichita during World War II with an Army baseball team and had wanted to bring a college team to play WU. He admitted before the game his squad could lose by 50 points.

He was a little optimistic.

CAN'T KEEP A GOOD MAN HERE

Jack Mitchell certainly had the popularity and knowledge to be a successful football coach in these parts. A four-sport star at Arkansas City High, he was an All-America quarterback at Oklahoma and was even voted the most popular sports figure in Oklahoma in 1948.

After short stints as an assistant at Tulsa and Texas Tech, the 29-year-old Mitchell was hired to get the Shockers back into bowl games on a consistent basis. His first team (1953) may have overachieved a bit, going 4-4-1 in what was perceived as a rebuilding year.

Things were certainly looking up in 1954, too. The Shockers finished 9-1, which still remains as the program's best record. Behind the passing of Jack Conway and running backs Jim Klisanin (a three-time All-Valley player) and Leroy Hinman, WU lost only to Denver 27-14, and the wins included some big ones: Oklahoma A&M, Cincinnati and Tulsa. The Shockers also won

Jim Klisanin was a three-time All-Valley running back.

their first Missouri Valley championship.

On Nov. 9, just before the end of the season, Wichita was so happy with Mitchell that the university signed him to a 10-year contract.

Two months later, he became the head coach at Arkansas.

Pete Tillman lasted two years as head coach, Chalmer Woodard three. From 1948 to 1968, WU had 10 football coaches. None lasted more than three years.

THE SHINING SIXTIES

Maybe Hank Foldberg would be the guy. He took over in 1960 and guided the Shockers to an 8-2 record, followed by another 8-2 mark, a seven-game winning streak, and a berth in the Sun Bowl in 1961. Both seasons, WU won the Valley title.

But before the Sun Bowl in December of 1961 – where WU lost to Villanova 17-9 – Foldberg announced he would leave the university to coach at Texas A&M. That's three bowl games, and before two of them the head coach announced his resignation before the game.

A Sunflower columnist lamented: "We will get another coach. We will win more football games."

He was right. Marcellino "Chelo" Huerta, who had played at Florida and coached at Tampa University, became the Shockers' 24th head coach in 1962.

CHELO'S SWEET MUSIC By 1963, WU was again demanding national recognition. The Shockers, led by quarterback Henry Schichtle, halfback Miller Farr and receiver Bob Long, were an offensive machine. They finished second in the nation in total offense, sixth in scoring.

Not only that, but the Shocker defense only gave up a school-best 863 rushing yards.

Although denied a postseason bowl bid, Wichita finished 7-2 with a 26-15 whipping of Tulsa and the MVC title, the last time the Shockers wore that crown.

"They were the finest football team Wichita ever had," Huerta told The Eagle-Beacon before the team's 20-year reunion. "It was a great pleasure because they were young people who gave a great effort. They were definitely the best team I ever coached."

SCRAMBLIN' HANK Schichtle was a big reason for the Shockers' success in 1963. After WU opened the campaign with a 33-13 victory at Arizona State, Sun Devils coach Frank Kush dropped a note to the WU sports information office.

"Henry Schichtle is one of the best scrambling quarterbacks I've ever seen. Time and again we had him

Roland Lakes, a two-time all-conference center from Parsons, played in 11 NFL seasons.

Hank Foldberg was 16-5 in two seasons before moving on to Texas A&M.

Patriots coach Bill Parcells was a Shocker player and coach in the 1960s.

Shocker QB John Eckman led the nation in passing yards (2,339) in 1966.

trapped, but he'd escape to pass or run against us. He's a good one. Regards, Frank Kush."

Coming to Wichita from Coffeyville, Schichtle established records in most quarterback categories before he became a member of the New York Giants. The records he still holds are career completion percentage (.555) and career passing efficiency (137.1).

SLIP-SLIDING AWAY The end of the 1960s marked maybe the worst era of Shocker football. Boyd Converse took over from George Karras in 1967 and went 2-7-1, but he was fired when the program was hit with a two-year probation after charges of improper inducements to WSU athletes and illegal out-of-season practices.

Eddie Kriwiel, one of the Shockers' best players in the late '40s and early '50s and coach of the powerful Wichita West High team, took over after Converse left but fared no better, going 0-10.

In 1969, the job went to Ben Wilson. His first season was tough – WSU won its opener over Utah State, then lost eight straight before recovering to beat rival Tulsa 28-12 in the finale.

QUIZ

27. Who's the assistant coach to the left of 1967 head coach Boyd Converse (middle)?

CELEBRATING CESSNA Just south of 21st Street on the northwest side of campus, Veterans Field was home of the football Shockers for more than 20 years. It seated 12,500 fans and was home to five Valley championship teams.

But in 1969, WSU and the community were thinking bigger. A fast-moving campaign, kicked off by Cessna Aircraft's $300,000 donation and later a $750,000 contri-

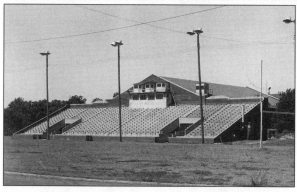

Cessna Stadium, above, opened in 1969 with an expansion cost of $1.5 million.

Shocker Stadium, left, was the school's first on-campus site, preceding Veterans Field.

Largest Cessna Stadium crowds:

30,518 Oklahoma State, 1978
30,055 Arkansas State, 1970
28,724 Kansas State, 1977
28,450 Tulsa, 1982
28,245 Utah State, 1969

bution from the student government, helped renovate the field into what became Cessna Stadium.

Stands on both the east and west sides of the field were extended far above Veterans Field's concrete base at a cost of $1.5 million. The grass was also converted to artificial turf, though that was changed back to grass by 1979.

Before Cessna Stadium or Veterans Field, WSU played its on-campus games at Shocker Stadium, located just east of the Henrion Gymnasium, which still stands on the southern part of the campus. Stands were built into the eastern part of the gym, and the Shockers played there until Veterans Field was dedicated on Thanksgiving Day, 1948.

THE UNIVERSITY'S DARKEST DAY

Enough can be written about Oct. 2, 1970 to fill this entire book and more. The plane crash that killed 31 Wichita State football players, coaches and boosters near Silver Plume, Colo., is easily the most recognizable day in the school's history. The nation may see WSU as a college baseball powerhouse or home to some nationally ranked basketball teams, but say "Wichita State" around any peripheral sports fan and the first reaction often will be, "The plane crash."

If you are old enough to remember Oct. 2, 1970, you will surely never forget that day.

This is not meant to be a comprehensive account of what happened that day, only a point to reflect on the effect the crash had on so many people.

THE DAY Residents in the Loveland ski area remember a beautiful Friday afternoon in October developing. It was sunny and about 60 degrees, a picture-perfect day.

The Wichita State football team was en route to Logan, Utah, for a Saturday game with Utah State. In two Martin 404 charter planes – one named Black, the other Gold – the team took off from Denver after refueling and

WSU President Clark Ahlberg holds a news conference after the crash.

The Athletic Department

Wichita State University

acknowledges with grateful appreciation

your kind expression of sympathy

Those who died on Oct. 2

Players
Marvin Brown, 19
Don Christian, 20
John Duren, 19
Ron Johnson, 21
Randy Kiesau, 20
Mal Kimmel, 21
Carl Krueger, 19
Steve Moore, 21
Tom Owen, 20
Gene Robinson, 21
Tom Shedden, 20
Richard Stines, 19
John Taylor, 21
Jack Vetter, 21

Staff and boosters
Bert Katzenmeyer, 52,
    athletic director
Marian Katzenmeyer, 52
Ben Wilson, 44, head coach
Helen Wilson, 44
Tom Reeves, 31, trainer
Marty Harrison, 19,
    team manager
Carl Fahrbach, 50,
    dean of admissions
Floyd Farmer, 35,
    ticket manager
Ray Coleman, 45,
    Shocker Club chairman

Maxine Coleman, 43
John Grooms, 42,
    won membership drive
Etta Mae Grooms, 38,
    won membership drive
Ray King, 48,
    state representative
Yvonne King, 41

Crew
Dan Crocker, 27, pilot
Judy Lane, 28,
    flight attendant
Judy Dunn, 39,
    flight attendant

headed to Logan.

The Black plane followed the flight plan by heading north to Laramie, Wyo., and gaining altitude before going west over the Rocky Mountains. But the Gold plane's pilots had decided to take a scenic route through the mountains west of Denver.

It turned into a tragic mistake. The National Transportation Safety Board determined that the pilots took the plane into a box canyon at too low an altitude. When it was apparent that the plane, which was cited as being 5,000 pounds overweight, wouldn't clear the

Coach Ben Wilson

mountains, the pilots attempted to turn the plane around, but the turn wasn't possible and the plane instead crashed into Mount Trelease.

Thirty-one of the 40 people on board died. Some of the survivors suffered burns before stumbling down the mountain for help. As they made their way down, the plane's nearly full fuel tanks exploded.

Those who died left behind 22 children and five wives. Thirteen of the children lost both parents.

THE AFTERMATH The Utah State game was canceled, as was the following Saturday's game with Southern Illinois. But the remaining players voted 76-1 to continue the season with an Oct. 24 game at ninth-ranked Arkansas.

It was called the Second Season.

John Hoheisel, a linebacker who survived the crash, led the Shockers onto the field that night in Little Rock. They didn't run, but walked solemnly behind their captain, who was on crutches.

Wearing black on the road in memory of lost teammates, two Shockers accompanied Hoheisel for the slow walk to the center of the field for the coin toss. As they moved forward, 40,000 Razorback fans gave them an emotional standing ovation. It moved Hoheisel to tears.

"That ovation was for the guys on that team that had the guts to go out and play again," Hoheisel told The Wichita

Twenty-two days after the crash, survivor John Hoheisel leads WSU onto the field in Little Rock to face Arkansas.

Eagle 20 years later. "It was for their Second Season."

WSU was no match for the mighty Razorbacks. Playing with many second-stringers and freshmen who had been given permission to play by the NCAA, the Shockers lost 62-0.

After the game, Arkansas players rushed to midfield to give WSU players hugs. The fans gave the Shockers another standing ovation.

"I'm sure the score could have been 100-0," Seaman said after the game. "Arkansas has a great, great football team. But I've got my own No. 1 team tonight."

WSU didn't win a game in the Second Season, but that didn't matter. The Shockers had tried to move on.

THE MOURNING From the hand-drawn card by the St. Mary's grade-school football team of Humboldt, Iowa, to the telegram from the Green Bay Packers, messages of sympathy poured into the university in the days and weeks after the crash.

Soon after National Transportation Safety Board hearings were being held on campus, a plane carrying the Marshall University football team crashed on Nov. 15. The two tragedies were combined into a "Night of Stars" benefit at Levitt Arena. Among the stars who donated their talents: Monty Hall, Bill Cosby, Kate Smith, Leif Erickson, Lou Rawls, Phil Ford and Mimi Hines, George Gobel, Minnie Pearl, Mac Davis, Marilyn Maye, The Young Americans and Gordon Jenkins. The telethon raised more than $157,000 for WSU.

John Hoheisel meets the Arkansas players before the coin toss.

Members of the Texas A&M team flew to Wichita to present the Shockers with $5,000, earmarked for the team's postseason banquet.

THE MOUNTAIN The scar still remains on Mount Trelease, high above I-70 west of Denver. Much of the twisted and charred metal litter the mountainside, with burned trees still standing tall though refusing to grow or produce new branches.

Because the crash happened before federal policy mandated that the wreckage be cleaned up, the site hasn't changed much since the crash. It can be reached by following a rugged, 45-minute trail that originally was cleared by bulldozers taking out important parts of the plane.

Below the site and a few hundred yards east on I-70 lies

Equipment was among the debris left by the plane crash on Oct. 2, 1970.

a bronze marker in memory to the people who died on Oct. 2. If motorists aren't looking for it, they'll never see it.

Listed are the 31 people who died, below an inscription which reads: "AS TIME GOES BY, MEMORIES FADE, BUT WE WILL NEVER FORGET."

TRYING TO REGROUP

Many believe the punch to the gut that the plane crash caused never allowed Wichita State to collect its collective football breath. Over the next 16 seasons, WSU had a winning record twice. But with some standout players and Ted Bredehoft at the athletic director's helm, it was never boring.

STARS OF THE '70S Randy Jackson, who would have a three-year NFL career, came back from the crash to lead WSU in rushing and scoring in 1971. That was also the first season for Rick Dvorak, a big defensive tackle from Spearville who would be a three-time All-Valley selection and the MVC defensive player of the year in 1972.

Nicknamed "Little Beaver" because of his Indian heritage, Sam Adkins became the Shockers' career passing leader with three terrific seasons from 1974-76. Adkins was only the second Shocker QB to complete more than 50 percent of his passes. Teammate Bryan Hanning was the school's receiving leader with 1,715 career yards.

Randy Jackson came back from the crash in 1971 to gain 820 yards.

Mickey Collins became WSU's career rushing leader, piling up 2,242 yards. On the defensive side in the late '70s, linebacker Brian Anderson was the Valley defensive player of the year in 1978.

BARNUM AND BAILEY BREDEHOFT Among the Bredehoft schemes to bring fans into Cessna Stadium during his 10-year tenure, 1972-82:
■ Camel races.
■ Money scrambles.
■ 25,000 yellow cricket clickers.
■ Reimbursement for season-ticket holders for games WSU lost at home.
■ Parachutists delivering the game ball.
■ Two-cent tickets, one-cent tickets, free tickets.
■ Turkey scrambles.
■ The Dallas Cowboy Cheerleaders.

Rick Dvorak was All-Valley for three seasons.

Another yard and Joe Williams (2) would have the NCAA record for longest field goal all to himself.

- Evel Knievel.
- Shocker Bread.
- Big Wu, a huge Shocker inflated to stand at the south end of the stadium.
- Fireworks.

IN THE RECORD BOOK WSU was wrapping up an easy 30-7 victory over Southern Illinois on Oct. 21, 1978, when place-kicker Joe Williams rushed to Coach Jim Wright and asked for a chance to kick a long field goal with four seconds left.

The distance: 67 yards, an NCAA record. But neither Williams nor Wright knew it would tie the mark of Arkansas' Steve Little and Texas' Russell Erxleben. So when Williams booted the ball from just beyond his own 43-yard line, he didn't know that another foot or so back and he'd have had the record all to himself.

"I'm being honest," Wright said after the game. "I didn't know how far it was."

Williams was certainly an unlikely candidate to be an NCAA record-holder. Born in East Berlin, he and his mother fled to the west before the Berlin Wall was erected. Born Joseph Hans Jurgen, he came to the United States in 1972 and was adopted by Delmar Williams, a career Air Force man, and his wife. He went to Gulf Coast junior college in Mississippi before he was spotted by Wright.

WILLIE HITS WICHITA

Williams' kick wasn't enough to save Wright's job. With Wright finishing 17-37-1 over five years, Bredehoft decided a change was necessary, and Willie Jeffries was his man.

Jeffries came to WSU as a highly successful coach at South Carolina State, a predominantly black college. He was 50-13-4 and came to Wichita as the first black coach at an NCAA Division I-A school.

28. Name the four Shockers who have had the longest NFL careers.

FACING THE BIG BOYS Bredehoft threw Jeffries into the fire early, scheduling games with such national powers as Alabama, South Carolina, Arizona State and Tennessee. The thought was that WSU would receive large guaranteed checks from playing at those places, which would help drive the program when home attendance was suffering.

The on-field results were mixed. WSU was outscored 111-0 in losses to Alabama and South Carolina, but it did play Arizona State within two touchdowns and lost to Tennessee only 24-21.

"One of these days, we're going to knock one of those big teams off," Bredehoft told The Eagle in 1981. Maybe so, but WSU struggled to just 10 wins in Jeffries' first three years.

RENEWING RIVALRIES Playing the powerhouses was fine, but some Shocker fans wanted their school playing sister schools Kansas and Kansas State. WSU had not met KU since 1946 and K-State since 1977.

A group called KOSMIK (Keep Our Sports Money in Kansas) formed to force Big Eight schools to meet Wichita State. They got their wish in 1982, though the group had nothing to do with the contracts. KU agreed to play WSU for three years beginning in 1982, while K-State agreed to games in 1982 and '85.

Boosted by Prince McJunkins at quarterback, Willie Jeffries had two of the school's most potent offensive teams in 1981 and 1982.

SETTING HIGHER GOALS Doug Schroeder's 39-yard field-goal attempt sailed high above the Cessna Stadium upright, a close-enough kick to go either way. But with the game on the line, officials ruled the attempt wide and Drake held on for a 24-23 victory in October 1981.

Days later, Bredehoft ordered that new, 12-foot longer goalposts be installed. The new posts reached the NFL standard height of 32 feet. "Anybody who kicks the ball above these goalposts should be awarded four points," Bredehoft said.

29. Who led the Shockers in punt returns in 1978?

1982: THE LAST HURRAH

Much was expected of the 1982 Shockers. After all, quarterback Prince McJunkins was the Valley's most exciting player and ready for his senior season. Tailback

THE NUMBER FIT THE PLAYER

At the family home in Muskogee, Okla., he would line chairs and sofas in an obstacle course alignment. The first chair might be the defensive end, the second chair the outside linebacker, and the sofa would be the free safety.

While so many other football players honed their skills on the practice field, Prince McJunkins' field was carpeted and his opponents upholstered.

"I guess the work at home paid off," he once said.

That's safe to say. As Wichita State's finest quarterback and maybe its best-ever player, McJunkins was as exciting a player as could be found.

"When the chips are down, Prince pulls you through," Willie Jeffries once said. "He plays electrifying football."

Running the Shockers' option offense, McJunkins had a blend of running skill, elusiveness and an ever-improving throwing arm that combined to do things that no quarterback had ever done in college football.

When McJunkins' career ended in 1982, he had thrown for 4,544 yards and rushed for 2,047. He was the first player in NCAA history to rush for 2,000 yards and pass for 4,000.

But numbers don't do McJunkins justice. Offensive coordinator Larry Beckish may have put it best in 1981.

"Hitting McJunkins is kind of like hitting a sack of flour that is open at one end," Beckish said. "He absorbs the blow and doesn't

Prince McJunkins' elusiveness made him the greatest quarterback in Shocker history.

take the brunt of it."

There were many instances of Prince's magic. The 50-yard touchdown pass to Don Dreher that beat Kansas was certainly one, and the time he scored twice in 12 seconds on option runs of 58 and 20 yards.

A two-time Valley offensive player of the year who finished as WSU's career leader in total offense by almost 3,000 yards, McJunkins joined Linwood Sexton as the only football players with retired jerseys.

No. 1 fit McJunkins like a glove.

Said defensive teammate Mike Johnston: "God, I'm glad when spring ball's over so I don't have to face him again."

Eric Denson, a transfer from Auburn, was a freshman who could step in right away and perform. Receiver Reuben Eckels was back and the perfect target for McJunkins. Matchups with intrastate rivals Kansas and Kansas State, as well as a home game with conference rival Tulsa, had Shocker fans salivating.

WSU delivered.

In its finest season since 1961, Wichita State finished 8-3, won four of five home games, set a Cessna Stadium single-season attendance record and got maybe the biggest victory in the history of the program.

PAIN IN THE GRASS After Cessna Stadium went back to a grass surface in 1979, the field most times looked like the "before" side of a how-to article in a lawn magazine.

But as the 1982 opener against Missouri-Rolla approached, it was in maybe its worst shape. A high-school All-Star game was played on it a month earlier, and The Eagle-Beacon's story referred to the field as "a 100-yard Mohawk haircut." WSU coaches privately called the grass "Astrodirt."

Ever the P.T. Barnum, though, Bredehoft tried to make the best out of a bad situation. He sent sports information director Kevin Weiberg onto the field to count the blades of grass. He wasn't kidding, either.

Prince McJunkins left WSU as the total offense leader.

"I was told when I went to work for Ted Bredehoft that there would be very few dull moments," Weiberg told The Eagle-Beacon. Weiberg actually got down and counted the blades in a square foot, then did some calculating from there.

The result? Approximately 94.5 million blades. The Eagle-Beacon, disputing the results, did its own count and estimated 27.2 million blades. As always, Bredehoft had an explanation: "We anticipated that because the field had been mowed."

'WE HAD THE HEART' Shocker fans had waited 36 years for a football meeting with Kansas and nine more since the last victory over the Hawks. And after 579 yards of offense and a 51-14 win over Missouri-Rolla in the opener, WSU was pumped.

"Are we as good as KU? I'd say they're as good as we are," McJunkins told The Eagle-Beacon the day before the game. "That's all we're hearing: Are we up to their standard? My question is this: Are they up to OUR standard?"

In front of a Memorial Stadium crowd of 41,500 – many wearing black and gold – Kansas looked good in the first half of its season opener and led 10-3. But this game was far from over.

Don Dreher heads to the end zone with the winning touchdown in WSU's 13-10 victory over Kansas.

In the second half, KU seemed to be losing steam. Wichita State still appeared fresh, as noted by both teams after the game. A Sergio Lopez-Chavero field goal cut KU's lead to 10-6, but the Shockers were still waiting with the knockout punch.

Late in the fourth quarter, they got it.

Starting at its own 16 with 4:35 to go, WSU went just 5 yards in two plays. But McJunkins hit Eckels for 29 yards on third down to put the ball at the 50.

Then came The Pass.

As McJunkins dropped back, split end Don Dreher took off up the right sideline. He beat his defender, and KU free safety Roger Foote was late helping out.

McJunkins lofted a high pass that Dreher caught at the 25 as he sprinted to the end zone. Foote met him short of the goal line as Dreher lept.

Touchdown. WSU snuffed out KU's last-ditch drive for the 13-10 victory and those invaluable bragging rights. And McJunkins' pre-game boast was on the money.

Bredehoft and Jeffries hugged on the field, then players tossed Jeffries into the locker-room showers. Once he came out, he made a statement that was on the minds of many Shocker fans that sunny Saturday.

"This is the biggest victory I've had since coming to Wichita and it could be the biggest victory for the entire history of Wichita State football," he said.

Dreher would have a solid yet unspectacular Shocker career. But ask WSU fans who caught The Pass, and they'll know. For Dreher, it was sweet justice.

"Kansas, they recruited me. But at the last minute I guess they decided they didn't want me," Dreher said. "Ever since then I have wanted to get back at them, and this is perfect timing."

Said KU's Foote, from Peabody: "We'll have to take a lot of crap now."

MAULED IN MANHATTAN Wichita State went to Manhattan with tons of confidence, but didn't come home the same way. With a season-low 231 yards of offense, WSU suffered its first loss after the Wildcats won 31-7 with 17 fourth-quarter points.

McJunkins took a pounding, suffering a concussion early in the fourth quarter. He already had three turnovers, two on interceptions and one on a fumble.

REGROUP FOR REWARDS Determined not to let the K-State loss put a damper on the future, Wichita State went on a wild four-game winning streak. First, there was 24-21 win at West Texas State, when the Buffaloes' Dennis Steinbock missed a 40-yard, game-tying field goal as time expired. "I've got to find something else to do for a

At 6-foot-7, James "Jumpy" Geathers was an imposing pass-rusher when he arrived in the face of a quarterback.

living," Jeffries said after the game.

Then there was McJunkins' best day ever, 351 yards of total offense in a 48-14 rout at Illinois State. After that was a 28-26, 992 yards-of-offense day against New Mexico State, then an easy 30-13 win at Texas-Arlington.

With the Valley title on the line the next week at home against Tulsa, WSU wasn't at full strength. McJunkins tried to play on a sprained ankle but had to sit most of the time. Backup Terry George hit Reuben Eckels for a 52-yard pass in the fourth quarter to cut Tulsa's lead to 27-21, but the Hurricane ate up clock and added a field goal to win the conference crown.

ONE FOR TED During the season, WSU announced that it had violated NCAA rules in the recruitment of a prospective football player, Dennis "Tex" Allen. The NCAA began an investigation in October and eventually handed down a probation sentence.

Amid NCAA troubles, Bredehoft appeared to be in trouble as athletic director. But on Nov. 6, the football team gave him a final send-off after its 38-29 victory at Drake.

Linemen Greg Blackman and David Unruh lifted Bredehoft onto their shoulders for a ride to the locker

Originally headed elsewhere, Eric Denson remembered a business card from Willie Jeffries and called when he wasn't happy at Auburn. He finished as WSU's career rushing leader.

room. "We wanted to dedicate this game to him," Jeffries said. "There's been some friction around the school and around our city. ... We thought it would perk him up a little. He's been down and out."

In the win – WSU's eighth of the season – McJunkins became the first player in NCAA history to pass for 4,000 yards and rush for 2,000. Denson also had a career-high 194 yards.

Two days later, Bredehoft resigned.

Ted Bredehoft delighted in the 1982 football season before he was forced to resign late in the year.

PRINCE'S FINAL DAY Laramie, Wyo., in November isn't a fun place. It's freezing cold, it snows, and if you're not used to the 7,220-foot altitude ...

That's the kind of final game it was for Wichita State. Trying for a nine-win season for the first time since 1954, the Shockers came close but lost to Wyoming 24-20. On a frozen artificial turf field, McJunkins and the rest of the Shockers' option game never got on track.

McJunkins wasn't at his best, anyway, feeling dizzy and missing the entire third quarter. "I would have really liked to have gone out a winner," McJunkins said. "We worked so hard the last four years to get to this point. We laid the groundwork for years to come."

Willie Jeffries listens, intently, as Athletic Director Lew Perkins discusses the decision to fire Jeffries with the media on Jan. 22, 1984.

JEFFRIES OUT Despite the departure of McJunkins to the Canadian Football League, there was still a ton of talent on the Shocker roster in 1983. Career rushing leader Denson was only a sophomore, and receiver Reuben Eckels was one of the university's all-time bests, catching passes for more than 2,000 yards.

In his first college head-coaching job, Ron Chismar wanted to build for long-range success.

But the season was a disappointment. WSU finished 3-8 starting 0-4 and including a 57-6 loss at Kansas and a 44-14 loss at Arizona State.

With an NCAA probation hanging over the program, Jeffries was fired after the season by new athletic director Lew Perkins and new university president Warren Armstrong. Jeffries left with a 21-32-2 record (.400) but the third-most victories on the WSU coaching chart and most in the modern era.

Now it was up to Ron Chismar. A 14-year college assistant at Bowling Green, Michigan State and Arizona State, Chismar took over WSU's program in his first head-coaching role.

WSU was 5-17 in Chismar's first two seasons, including a 16-10 win at Kansas State in 1985.

"I don't claim to be an architect or know anything about planning a building," Chismar once said. "But I honestly think the thing that is so drastically needed here is a solid-based program. That has been lacking for a long, long period of time."

THE END

Sept. 6, 1986, was a beautiful Saturday in Wichita. The sun was out and hopes were high in Cessna Stadium. Hopes that this would be a turn-around year for Wichita State football.

"I think it's time for us to make our move," Chismar said before the season. "We've spent a couple years struggling; now I think it's time for us to come back out on the other end."

WSU sure looked great in a 69-6 whomping of San Francisco State in the opener. It was the most points a Shocker team had racked up since the opening game in 1954, and that team won nine games. Nobody cared that San Francisco State had a program without scholarships.

And on that sunny Saturday, probably nobody in the stadium could ever have imagined that in less than three months, the Shocker program would end.

LOWEST OF THE LOWS Just as the words "Don Dreher" bring a smile to a Shocker fan's face, "Morehead State" prompts a shake of the head.

Few fans had ever heard of the Division I-AA college from Kentucky before the Eagles met WSU in Cessna Stadium on Sept. 20, 1986. They certainly acted like a I-AA patsy, falling behind 35-3 at halftime. With 88-degree temperatures and strong south winds, less than diehard fans may have left early to beat traffic.

They were the smart ones. In the 30-minute second half, Morehead State scored 33 points and beat WSU 36-35 to record the greatest comeback in the history of college football.

Brian McDonald made the transition from option-style quarterback to drop-back passer, finishing as the Shockers' career passing yardage leader.

"I've been in coaching for 30 years and I have never, ever, ever lost a ball game like this," Chismar said. "It's a disgrace."

Anything Morehead tried worked. Eighteen third-quarter points had the Eagles back in the game. Still, WSU led 35-21 with 2:25 to play. But gains of 23, 27 and

30 yards led to a Morehead touchdown just 31 seconds later, making it 35-28.

Then Morehead recovered a beautiful onside kick, scoring seven plays later. After such a startling comeback, Morehead was content to kick the extra point and go home with a tie, but Charlie Stepp's kick was wide.

The Shockers, though, were offsides on the play. Feeling lucky this time, Morehead went for two and got it when quarterback Adrian Breen ran in the conversion.

"I have never seen such a turn of events in my life," Chismar said.

1897-1986 Seventeen days later, the press conference was called.

"I have reached the painful conclusion – and it is doubly difficult and painful for me because of my love of college football – that I must suspend the football program immediately and indefinitely unless the $3.6 million required for its continuance is immediately forthcoming," President Warren Armstrong said.

The financial help didn't come. WSU football had lost too much money (it finished with an $839,000 deficit) and too little community interest to keep going, and Armstrong followed a recommendation from a company that studied sports management systems.

A somber Chismar and Perkins spoke of their disap-

WSU was 3-8 in its final season, beating San Francisco State, Tulane and Central Florida.

University President Warren Armstrong blamed a lack of community support and increasing athletic department deficits.

pointment. Chismar said he understood Armstrong's decision, though he didn't feel he or his staff had been given a chance to build a winner.

Coaches from around the country invaded Wichita like vultures picking at the meat off a carcass. Fifty-three Shockers had eligibility remaining and most went elsewhere to play. They were immediately eligible.

"What happened to me today and what happened to my kids is the worst thing I've ever been through," Chismar said.

"I'm frustrated, there's no question," Perkins said. "I think we gave it a hell of a shot. Maybe football was not meant to be at Wichita State."

Eighty-nine years of black and gold memories may disagree.

WSU's Other Stars

They are the "other" sports, the "non-revenue" sports, the "Olympic" sports. Whatever the terminology, they are the teams that play in front of 10 or 100 fans instead of 10,000.

Wichita State has a rich tradition in many of these sports, such as men's tennis, men's track and field and men's and women's bowling. Those teams have developed numerous conference champions, All-Americans and even national champions. Still, they don't get the banner headlines or even a fraction of the athletic department budget that the men's basketball or baseball teams get.

But they put in the same amount of work and dedication. And just maybe they play a little more for the love of the sport. After all, in almost all cases there is no shot at big money in professional sports, nor are there the cheers from thousands of fans on a nightly basis. It's the sport.

Here's a look at some Shockers you may not know much about.

WOMEN'S BASKETBALL

SHOWING UP THE GUYS Which came first, the women or the men?

Women's basketball. Really.

Women's hoops at Fairmount College actually originated 25 days before men's basketball during the 1905-06 school year, and immediately enjoyed more success than the men.

The 1910 Fairmount women's team finished 7-0 and was crowned, unofficially, the Kansas champions.

Fairmount's first game, on Jan. 6, 1906, was a 16-13 loss to Wichita High School. But as the season continued, Fairmount won 5 of 7 games and outscored oppo-

nents 135-91. The other loss was a 15-7 decision to Cooper College, a game played in an opera house.

Early games were played under "women's rules," which allowed six players on each team, with three on each side of the midcourt line. Three players were for defense only, and they would move the ball across the line to three forwards whose only job was to score baskets.

The Fairmount women were regarded as four-time unofficial state champions (the men, meanwhile, were 3-10 and wouldn't have their first winning season until a year later). Led by captain Jessie Wilson and forward Pauline Grafton, Fairmount won all seven of its games, including an 86-21 margin in its final three contests.

RESTARTING THE PROGRAM
About 20 women showed up at Henrion Gymnasium on Oct. 25, 1974, maybe not knowing what they were getting themselves into. Some were volleyball players, some were curious, and some were wanting the chance to play college basketball.

Wichita State had resumed a women's basketball program.

Larry Thye, a university physical education instructor, was the coach. He was paid a pittance ($3,300) and worked without any assistant coaches.

An easy job? Forget it.

WELCOME TO INTERCOLLEGIATE ATHLETICS
WSU's first taste of games came at Enid, Okla., in the three-game Phillips Invitational. The Shockers opened with three devastating losses: 100-16 to Phillips, 79-39 to Oklahoma State and 80-32 to Wayland Baptist.

Give the Shockers credit, though, since they went home and won two straight, over McPherson College and Washburn. WSU finished 4-13 in the first season.

MIGHTY MARGUERITE
Wichita State got better quickly, though, and much of it was due to one player. Marguerite Keeley, a 6-foot-1 center who had such a nice shooting touch that she often played forward, joined the Shockers from Independence Community College and immediately made an impact.

In 1975-76, Keeley led the Shocks to an 11-7 record. She averaged 18.2 points, 15.5 rebounds and shot 51.6 percent from the field. Keeley was even better in her senior season, averaging 22.4 points, 13 boards and shooting an amazing 60.5 percent. Five of WSU's eight 20-rebound games are Keeley's, and almost 20 years after her career ended she is still in the top 10 in seven statistical categories. Pretty amazing when you consider she played half the games of most other Shockers on the lists.

Keeley went out in style, too, scoring 30 points in her final game, a loss to nationally ranked Phillips University.

30. *During her season in the women's pro league, Marguerite Keeley was traded from the Milwaukee Does to what team?*

Marguerite Keeley (31) had 17 or more rebounds in nine games over a two-year period.

Kathryn Bunnell recruited hard in Kansas and came up with some top recruits.

LOADED WITH TALENT Keeley's departure was felt for a couple of seasons, and back-to-back 6-20 records were the result. But Coach Kathryn Bunnell took over in 1978 and Shocker fortunes began to change.

The 1980-81 roster was full of potential. Career scoring leader Terry O'Bryon, 6-foot-6 Theresa Dreiling and hot-shot Kem Strobel were all back, as well as tenacious rebounder Pam Mattingly and steady guard Kathy Garofalo.

But what excited the program's followers even more was the pickup of the two blue-chippers from the Wichita City League, Kapaun Mount Carmel's Mary Kennedy and Heights' Paula Redo. It equated to as big a recruiting coup as the WSU men had pulled off in 1981, getting Greg Dreiling and Aubrey Sherrod from the same high schools.

At 6-foot-5, Kennedy teamed with former Kapaun teammate Dreiling and the 6-1 Mattingly to give WSU a huge front line. Redo, a flashy point guard who could also shoot, turned out to be WSU's leading scorer.

"When the talent we have now matures together, I think we'll be able to play with anybody," Bunnell said.

Terry O'Bryon led WSU in scoring just once in four years, but still finished her career as the scoring leader.

A GOOD TRANSFUSION Bunnell used nine players regularly and the depth showed. Beginning the season ranked in the top 30 and scoring a school-record 74.7 points a game, the Shockers won 9 of their last 10 and beat Kansas State in a playoff game. Despite a loss to Minnesota in the Association of Intercollegiate Athletics for Women Region VI tournament in Minneapolis, WSU finished 20-11, easily the school's best record. O'Bryon and Redo earned All-Region VI honors.

"I think we've established our program," Bunnell said. "We did what we wanted to do even though we waited until the last minute to do it."

O'Bryon, a 5-8 swingman from Baldwin, finished her career with 1,425 points, a school best that would stick for another five seasons. In her four years, WSU improved from 6-20 to 20-11.

TRANSITION TIMES The end of the 1982-83 season brought a few changes. Bunnell left after five seasons, WSU was ready to begin play in the newly formed Gateway Conference, and the Shockers would begin a string of 10 years without a winning record.

The one constant was Lisa Hodgson, who came from Nickerson and was a role player in the 1980-81 season.

Theresa Dreiling (left) and Mary Kennedy formed WSU's Twin Towers.

Three times, Lisa Hodgson led WSU in scoring.

After averaging less than four points that year, Hodgson became a star the next three years. A consistent 47-percent shooter from the outside, she entered her senior season within reach of O'Bryon's scoring record.

Before her final game, Hodgson needed 16 points to set the record. With 23 seconds to play and the game decided against Drake, she needed 12 more points. Head coach Karen Harden told her huddled players, "We're going to do this one for Lisa."

Not enough time, though. Hodgson made a basket at the buzzer, but ended one point shy of O'Bryon. "It seemed like it just buzzed by," Hodgson said after the game. "It was short but sweet." Nevertheless, Hodgson is among WSU career leaders in nine categories and was a two-time All-Gateway pick.

POINTS FROM PITTSBURGH While Hodgson was the standout, Allison Daniel waited in her shadow for her shot.

Daniel, a 5-8 guard from Pittsburgh who was one of Pennsylvania's best high school players in the early '80s, had a solid first two seasons at WSU, averaging 11.1 points.

Once she was called upon to handle the scoring load, Daniel responded with almost 20 points a game as a junior and almost 18 as a senior. And, unlike Hodgson, Daniel didn't wait until the final game of her career to try to break

Allison Daniel started her last 83 games in a Shocker uniform and holds the school scoring record with 1,638 points.

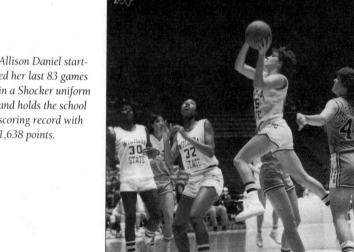

the school scoring record. She scored a career-high 31 points against Northern Iowa on Jan. 24, 1986, hitting 13 of 17 shots and moving past Hodgson and O'Bryon on the same basket.

But Daniel, a two-time All-Gateway selection, was just as proud of her defensive abilities. She averaged more than two steals a game, finishing with a school-record 246 (more than any WSU men's player, too). "That's something for a kid who is such an offensive player," Harden said.

WATCHING, WAITING During the 1970s and most of the '80s, while Wichita State struggled to four winning seasons in 15 years, Linda Hargrove was about 50 miles to the south in Arkansas City. She observed the building of the Shocker program, both the good times and bad.

Hargrove knew all about building a program. Asked to begin a women's basketball team at Cowley County Community College and not knowing much about the sport, she strived to learn about the game and coaching at the college level.

"When I first started coaching it, I didn't know anything about it," Hargrove said. "I can remember reading books and going home and asking (her husband) Ed to tell me the difference between a pick and a screen. Then we'd get in the kitchen and he'd show me the difference."

So when Harden resigned in 1989, Hargrove knew it was time to try it at Wichita State. Applying for a third time, she was hired.

Hargrove hoped to build as quickly and successfully as she did at Cowley County, where she won 73.8 percent of

31. At Cowley County, what was Linda Hargrove's coaching record against WSU?

Linda Hargrove has steadily built the WSU women's basketball program into a consistent winner.

*In 1994-95, Ann
Hollingsworth (25)
became the Shocker
program's seventh
1,000-point scorer.*

her games, including an incredible 137-12 Jayhawk Conference record since the conference formed in 1978.

Hargrove actually was a track-and-field star. Originally from Udall, she competed in the 1968 U.S. Olympic Trials in the hurdles but didn't qualify. At Cowley, she also coached women's track, volleyball (three conference titles) and softball.

"My background as an athlete is not in women's basketball. It's in track and field," Hargrove said at a news conference announcing her hiring in 1989. "In high school we didn't have an opportunity to play women's basketball, or I'm sure I would have."

In 17 years at Cowley, Hargrove had only one losing season and won 20 games in 10 of her final 12 years. She also received Coach-of-the-Year honors in her last three seasons (and beat WSU 71-63 in 1978).

But, as Hargrove figured, making WSU a 20-game winner was no easy task. The Shockers won only seven in her first season, six in her second.

"At Cowley, I just took the wins for granted," Hargrove once told The Eagle. "I just remembered the

losses, and very few of the wins."

The wins started coming in 1991-92. Behind Kareema Williams and what might be the finest season ever from a Shocker (20.9 points, 57.1-percent shooting, Missouri Valley Player of the Year and Newcomer of the Year), WSU won 13 games. Over the next three years, WSU had a 48-34 record, which included three consecutive winning seasons for the first time in school history.

Hargrove's drive is also apparent on the national basketball scene. She has been on numerous national boards as well as an assistant coach on two U.S. national teams.

Kareema Williams played only one season but was the Gateway Player of the Year in 1991-92.

ANN THE ACE One of Hargrove's most steady performers over four years was Ann Hollingsworth, a 6-foot All-State forward from Manhattan. Named All-Missouri Valley in her last three seasons, Hollingsworth became the Shockers' seventh 1,000-point scorer, ending at No. 4 with 1,272 points.

There's not much doubt about Hollingworth's consistency. She finished in the WSU career top 10 in 12 categories: points, scoring average, field goals and attempts, shooting percentage, free throws and attempts, free-throw percentage (first), rebounds, assists, steals and games played.

TENNIS

STAN'S PLAN The players come and go after a few seasons, but there's one common thread that binds all Wichita State men's tennis players.

They win. Often.

From 1978 to 1989, in fact, the Shocker men won the Missouri Valley Conference team championship every year. Since 1975, WSU has produced 57 singles champions and 27 doubles champions.

It was all part of Stan Kardatzke's grand scheme to make Wichita State a powerhouse in college tennis.

Kardatzke, a Wichita physician, took over the WSU program in 1978 with the goal of increasing the program's visibility, pumping up the budget and drawing top college players to Wichita as Shockers.

"I really don't know why I became so dedicated to the Wichita State tennis program," Kardatzke told The Eagle-Beacon in 1981. "I ask myself that quite often. My wife asks, too."

Whatever the reason, Kardatzke knew what he was doing. He coached the Valley champs in '78 and '79, then took an advisory role when Rex Coad assumed the coaching job in 1980.

Why the success? There's a simple formula: Get the best players possible, no matter where they're from.

When college tennis became popular in more places besides California and Texas, those newer programs, or

Stan Kardatzke's first WSU team (1978) won 19 of 23 dual matches, the Shockers' best record ever.

maybe only the ones that were more successful, realized that the best American players were being gobbled up by those Sun Belt schools.

So foreign countries became the unharvested crop for talent.

"The best amateur tennis in the world is college tennis," Coad once told The Eagle-Beacon. "If you're a talented foreign player, you want to come to an American college because that's the best deal going."

WSU recognized that before many competitors. Most Shocker tennis rosters are filled with players from Europe or South America.

THE FIRST TENNIS STAR Kardatzke's plan, actually, wasn't totally new. The Shockers' first tennis standout, Ben Anzola, was from Bogota, Colombia.

Unable to speak English when he arrived at WU, Anzola quickly became a national force. He finished fifth in the 1964 NCAAs, behind future stars such as Arthur Ashe and Marty Riessen.

*Rex Coad was a big
winner at WSU, as a
player and a coach.*

LOCAL BOY DOES GOOD One of WSU's greatest players
was Coad himself. After graduating from Wichita West
High, Coad joined the Shocker program just as it was
preparing to take off.

Coad won 104 singles matches, still a school record,
and was the team's MVP for three years. He won the No. 5
singles in the Valley in 1978 and qualified for the NCAA
doubles championships with Mark McMahon that year.

His success carried over to coaching. All nine of
Coad's Shocker teams, from 1980-88, won the conference championship. Of all the Shocker greats, Coad has
been in the middle of winning more than any of them.

"I could go around saying I'm a great coach and this
and that," Coad once said. "But my job basically is to help correct whatever minor problems
these players have."

Ground strokes were a big asset for Roberto Saad, a three-time Valley champion.

SAAD SITUATION Roberto Saad came to Wichita
State with a ton of credentials, though he didn't
know anything about the Shocker
program initially.

A two-time member of
Argentina's Junior Davis Cup
team, Saad was living with his
family in Pittsburgh when he decided to send
letters to top tennis universities, hoping for a
scholarship.

WSU was one of the few schools to write back.

Good move. From 1980 to 1984, Saad won
86 singles matches and during his junior season
reached as high as 11th in the national rankings.
A great baseline player, Saad in 1983 became the
first Shocker to reach the quarterfinals of the
NCAA singles championships and the first to
win three MVC No. 1 singles titles.

WIMBLEDON'S SHOCKER Andy Castle had never played
anything longer than a three-set match at Seminole (Fla.)
Junior College or at Wichita State, where he was one of
the Shockers' top players from 1983 to 1985.

So what was he doing in the second round at
Wimbledon, beating second seed Mats Wilander in a
five-set 1986 thriller? Maybe fulfilling a dream. Castle, a
wild-card entry with a serve-and-volley game suited for
grass, grew up in Somerset, England, but was unknown
to the British because he had spent time improving his
game in the U.S.

After the victory, Castle was asked about his spunk
and guts. He told the assembled media, "If ever you've
seen Wichita State play KU in basketball, that rubs off."

As Sports Illustrated's Frank Deford observed, "Castle

Andy Castle never won an MVC singles crown, but he pulled off WSU's biggest professional win.

explained (that) to a befuddled British and world press that didn't have the foggiest idea what this Kay-Yew thing was."

Jay Louderback's women's teams never finished below second in the Valley.

Jill Braendle (left) and Sandy Sadler won the Gateway Conference doubles titles the three times they entered.

ANYTHING YOU CAN DO... Shocker women's tennis has enjoyed similar success as the men over the years. WSU won its sixth conference championship in 1995, including two in a row. In 14 years of conference play, the Shockers have never finished below third.

Much of the credit goes to Jay Louderback, himself a Shocker player in the mid-'70s who was the women's coach from 1980 to 1986. WSU took three firsts and two seconds in conference play under Louderback.

OPPOSITES ATTRACT Women's standouts Sandy Sadler and Jill Braendle were as different on the court as possible.

Braendle, a left-hander who later became WSU's coach for three seasons, was the excitable partner, hitting the ball harder and burying the big shots. Sadler, a righty, was Miss Consistent, never getting too emotional or making unforced errors.

"Win or lose, she always has the same expression," Louderback said of Sadler. "She has won some big matches, and at times I think I am more excited than she is."

Together for three years, Sadler and Braendle won three Gateway Conference No. 1 doubles titles and were once ranked No. 1 nationally. They also twice qualified for the NCAA Doubles Championships.

Alone, Sadler won the Gateway No. 1 singles title all

four years and qualified once for the NCAAs. In 1990, she was named to the Gateway's All-Decade team.

The $1 million Coleman Tennis Complex on the Wichita State campus, built in 1993.

TRACK & FIELD/CROSS COUNTRY

HERM'S HARRIERS He often worked 20-hour days, with a meager budget and only a part-time assistant coach here and there. Besides coaching WSU's track and cross country teams, he took on every other job involving the two sports in Wichita, including drawing one of the best national track meets to Cessna Stadium on a yearly basis.

All that, and his teams were always among the best in the Midwest. Basically, Herm Wilson got things done.

Coaching at Wichita State from 1967 to 1983, Wilson was the rock on which the Shockers built a top-notch program in the 1970s. Recruiting Kansas stars such as long jumper Preston Carrington and distance runner Randy Smith, Wilson helped build Wichita into a hotbed of track.

"You like to feel like you serve in some way," Wilson once told The Eagle-Beacon. "I just hope we help the athletes in some small way. And the ultimate thing is to help the program at Wichita State, and to help the city of Wichita, through track and field. We've only begun."

No one coached longer at WSU, and Wilson helped the Shockers to five consecutive Missouri Valley cross country titles from 1971 to 1975.

Wilson resigned in 1983 after philosophical differences with new athletic director Lew Perkins, but his final list of credits included 81 individual conference champions, nine NCAA All-Americans, six Olympic Trials participants and one Olympian (Carrington).

Herm Wilson coached at WSU for 16 years, in one stretch leading the Shockers to five consecutive men's cross country championships.

WU'S FIRST CHAMPION Stomach cramps were bothering him so much he almost decided to quit halfway through the race. But soon they went away, and Harold Manning kept circling that Milwaukee track in 1930, heading toward WU's first national championship.

Manning won the national collegiate two-mile race in 9:18.1, becoming the university's first champion in any national intercollegiate event.

But getting there was half the fun for Manning. Growing up in nearby Sedgwick, he wasn't thought of as a distance runner until one day late in his senior season. Running against his teammates in a relay, he ran a mile in 4:44, a great time in that era. Soon after, Manning won the state high school mile and traveled to Chicago thanks to Sedgwick merchants who payed for his trip to win the national high school mile. WU coaches quickly offered him a scholarship.

Manning would get more noteriety, though, as he set his goals higher. He figured to qualify in the steeplechase for the 1932 Olympic Games in Los Angeles but finished seventh, one place away from qualifying.

Harold Manning was the university's first national champion and also its first Olympian.

"I took a coach train (to Palo Alto, Calif., for the trials), three days and two nights sitting up. I couldn't sleep," Manning told The Eagle-Beacon in 1989. "That's the only excuse I can think of. I thought I was in pretty good shape when I left here. Second or third day, it hit me and I was kinda numb."

Manning was still going strong in 1936, though, setting a world record at the Olympic Trials in New York.

But a wet and windy day for the steeplechase finals at the Games in Berlin was to Manning's disadvantage, because he had perfected the technique of hurdling the barriers instead of stepping on them. Slick approaches slowed his momentum and Manning finished fifth.

LONG JUMP LONG SHOT Preston Carrington was an outstanding basketball player and track performer at Topeka High, so much so that he came to Wichita State to play both sports.

As a point guard, he was good, averaging double figures both seasons after transferring from Butler County Community College. As a long jumper and triple jumper, though, he was great.

A two-time All-American in the long jump, Carrington ended his career as a Shocker and began a new one, a quest to qualify for the 1972 Olympic Games in Munich.

With help from supporters, Carrington established himself at some of the country's top meets before the U.S. Olympic Trials in Eugene, Ore., where he finished third in the long jump and with a place on the American Olympic team.

Accompanied by Wilson, Carrington went with the U.S. team in July 1972 and had the best jump in the preliminaries, leaping a personal-best 26 feet, 11 3/4 inches, the fourth-best jump in Olympic history.

"It was my final effort and I fouled in my first two," Carrington told The Eagle when he returned to the U.S. "I guess that I was nervous and that helped. I had laughed when Coach (Wilson) told me I could do 27 feet. He said, 'Don't laugh, you can.' "

"I had a good series of jumps, but I couldn't quite get it all together," said Carrington, who later changed his name to Syed Abdul Mufti.

ONE STEADY SHOCKER By far the most decorated Shocker track and field man was Randy Smith, who from 1971 to 1975 won 12 Missouri Valley championships in track and cross country.

From Wichita East High, Smith was a terrific distance runner, whether he was competing on an oval track or over a rugged cross country course. He burst on the national scene even as a freshman, qualifying for the NCAA championships in the 3,000-meter steeplechase, an event he would win three times at the Valley championships.

Smith would also win two Valley cross country titles, three three-mile runs, one mile run and three indoor crowns.

His best finish nationally was at the 1975 NCAAs, where he took second in the steeplechase. Smith also finished a school-best 10th at the NCAA cross country championships in 1974.

A year after his WSU career ended, Preston Carrington placed fifth in the long jump at the 1972 Munich Games.

The steeplechase was just one of the events that Shocker All-American Randy Smith excelled at.

LEAPING LONG AND HIGH Growing up in Council Grove, Connie Long quickly realized that she might have a future in high jumping.

In 1989, Connie Long was named an All-America high jumper both indoors and outdoors.

"I started beating the boys," she said. "They didn't like it, but the coaches did. And I think when you're good at something, you keep doing it and keep getting better."

Starting in the eighth grade, Long worked with a

long-term goal of competing in the Olympics. She never made it, coming as close as the 1992 U.S. Olympic Trials, but she did establish herself as Wichita State's greatest female track athlete.

Six times, Long qualified for either the NCAA's indoor or outdoor championships, earning All-America honors three times. Her best NCAA finish came in the 1989 NCAA outdoor meet, where she jumped 6 feet, 3/4 inches to finish second. That came after a school-record jump of 6-1 1/4 at the Gateway Conference meet, a competition she won five times (three outdoor, two indoor). Also that season, she finished fourth in the NCAA indoors.

"I was a woman possessed for a while," Long said.

GOLF

STRAIGHT-SHOOTING STEVENS They called him "Slim" because of his wiry body, a string bean with the prettiest of golf swings. He'd hit a ball long and straight and usually make something happen on the scorecard.

There are plenty of golfing legends around Wichita, but Johnny Stevens is as big as any of them. Still a force in local tournaments, Stevens gave a boost to Shocker golf in the 1960s.

Three times, he qualified for the NCAA championships. He twice won Missouri Valley medalist honors. His other accomplishments, ranging from state high school champ to touring professional, would take pages and pages to list.

If Stevens ever stops playing golf, and that's hard to imagine, the Stevens name will move on in golfing circles. Daughter Cathy is the women's coach at Wichita State, and son Charley has played on the PGA's Mini-Tour.

WSU'S GLUE Al Littleton resigned as Wichita State's golf coach in 1995, marking an end to an almost 50-year association with the university.

Littleton grew up in Wichita and, after returning from World War II, enrolled at WU in 1946. His excellence in golf was immediately noticable, as he was named captain of the Shocker squad for four years. All four seasons, he was All-Valley.

After 15 years away from the university, though, Littleton wanted back in Shocker Country. Following a stint as Crestview Country Club pro, he was named Shocker coach in 1973 and held the position until 1982, then took over again in 1989.

In that time, Littleton coached teams to three Valley championships, six NCAA appearances and tutored three All-Americans. Unlike the tennis program, which recruited all over the world, Littleton specialized at get-

QUIZ

32. What two players have the best WSU finish at the NCAA men's golf championships?

At the 1977 MVC Tournament, WSU's five golfers (Mike Caster, Matt Seitz, Bob Pancratz, Mike Shepard and Don Lee) were at or under par in 10 of 20 rounds.

Al Littleton was a four-time all-conference player and a longtime WSU coach.

ting the best homegrown players all while working part-time at the job. Other nationally prominent golf coaches worked full-time and made upwards of $50,000.

More than accomplishments, though, Littleton was one of the friendliest and most popular coaches and teaching professionals around. He was inducted into the Shocker Hall of Fame in 1990.

Natasha Fife was given the task of beginning a women's athletic program.

LEADING THE WOMEN'S CHARGE Truth be told, the greatest women's golfer at Wichita State never played one round for the school. But Natasha Fife certainly made her mark in the Shocker athletic department.

One of the state's best amateur golfers in the 1950s and 1960s, Fife was the first director of women's athletics at WSU, beginning in 1974. Given a meager budget of about $49,000 for all sports, Fife's dream, which started in a two-story house that held the women's offices, was to make WSU women's athletics on a par with the Kansas and Kansas States of the college scene.

Did it work? Sometimes. Basketball, the cornerstone of the WSU women's programs, competed well with its bigger sister schools. Other programs with less noteriety, such as softball and volleyball, also grew.

All the while, though, funding and emphasis grew for the women. Separated from the men's programs from 1974 to 1980, the women's budget grew six-fold in that time.

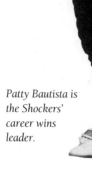

Patty Bautista is the Shockers' career wins leader.

SOFTBALL

'HELLO, COACH?' This was not the way it was supposed to be for Jim Maynard. Coaching the WSU softball team in his first season, he was lying in bed with a form of hepatitis while the Shockers played in the Gateway Conference tournament two states away.

"It's the toughest thing I've ever done," he told The Eagle-Beacon. "You just sit here and wait for the phone to ring, and then you're afraid to answer it."

When he did, though, he heard what he wanted to hear. Wichita State won three games on the final day, including two shutouts of winner's bracket champ Indiana State, to win the tournament for the first and only time. That, and the Shockers' automatic entry into the NCAA Tournament, was the biggest moment in WSU softball.

Maynard, a well-known figure in Wichita-area softball, was the perfect fit for the Wichita

State job. Having good ties to area high school and amateur programs, he recruited locally and in seven years has the only winning record of any WSU softball coach. His teams have won more than 20 games all seven years, a feat achieved only twice before his arrival in 1989.

QUIZ

33. *What category did the 1994 WSU softball team lead the nation in?*

VOLLEYBALL

NET RESULTS Wichita State volleyball has experienced many ups and downs over the years. The downs are unmistakable (that 0-33-1 record from 1980 still smarts), and the ups sometimes hard to come by.

But by Coach Phil Shoemaker's sixth year, 1988, the Shockers were making strides. Getting standout players such as hitters P.J. Barrett, Terri Brown, Janelle Watton and Kristin Carr, along with setter Yu-Chyi Yang, Wichita State achieved five straight winning seasons and a 108-63 record. Over a seven-year span, 12 Shockers earned all-conference recognition.

SET IN HER WAYS Yu-Chyi Yang came to the United States when she was 13, moving with her family to Wichita from Taiwan. She knew little English, couldn't communicate with teachers or classmates, and certainly didn't have any knowledge or interest in volleyball.

Until one day when her Wichita Heights physical education instructor noticed her volleyball skills. That led to Yang's playing for the Falcons, then earning a scholarship to Wichita State.

As a Shocker, Yang became the school's best setter ever, earning All-Gateway Conference honors in 1991 while helping WSU to a 25-13 record. That year, Yang contributed a record 1,559 assists.

Yu-Chyi Yang set up teammates more than 1,500 times in her 1991 all-conference season.

BOWLING

NO. 1, AGAIN AND AGAIN To put the Wichita State bowling program in perspective, you have do some big-time imagining:

Gordon Vadakin doesn't have to go out to recruit; the recruits come to him.

Picture WSU's basketball players jumping for joy in a mega-arena somewhere, celebrating the school's third straight national championship. Oh sure, the Shockers are in the Final Four every year, but three straight titles? Even that's impressive.

Then picture the women's basketball team making the NCAA Tournament every year, most years making the Final Four and winning the whole thing more than any other school.

Get the idea? If bowling were basketball, Wichita State's programs would be the dynasty of all dynasties.

But bowling isn't basketball. The hoopsters don't practice with the sounds of video games, billiard games and jukeboxes ringing in their ears as the bowlers do in the Campus Activity Center.

The hoopsters have a seven-figure budget supported by the athletic department and the NCAA. The bowlers don't get a sniff of the athletic budget and are funded by the CAC and fund-raisers.

The hoopsters, for all of their tradition, don't have bowling's success at WSU, either. Check out this success:

Rick Steelsmith went from the WSU bowling team to the PBA Tour.

■ In 1995, the men's team won a third straight national championship and fifth overall. It finished in the top three every year from 1986 to '95.

■ The women have won six national titles and have been at the national championships 20 of 21 years.

■ In 1994, WSU became the first school to win both sides of the national title in the same year.

■ For years now, the WSU program has been at a stature where aspiring bowlers come from all over the country – heck, all over the world – to try out for a precious spot on the team. High school bowlers read national publications that tout the Shockers' successes and, more often than not, call Coach Gordon Vadakin before he calls them.

Vadakin, himself a Shocker in the '70s, took over the program and made it sparkle. Stressing the mental aspect of the game over physical, he has produced two touring professionals, Rick Steelsmith and Justin Hromek, and others who have become coaches of international teams.

"In a way, we're more known on the national level than local," Vadakin said. "People at nationals are somewhat in awe of us. When they see us at nationals they say, 'WSU is back again, what are they going to win this year?' "

By the Numbers

All statistics are through the 1994-95 school year

SHOCKER SPORTS HALL OF FAME

Charlie Adams, administrator, 1949-74
Sam Adkins, football, 1974-76
Ben Anzola, tennis, 1964-66
Lindsey Austin, football, 1922-26
Carnot Brennan, football, 1913-17
Harold Brill, football, 1935-38
Greg Brummett, baseball, 1986-89
Fred Burton, track, 1965-67
Antoine Carr, basketball, 1979-83
Preston Carrington, track-basketball, 1969-71
Joe Carter, baseball, 1979-81
Red Coad, tennis, 1973-78, coach, 1980-88
Sheldon Coleman, at-large
Harry Corbin, administrator, 1949-63
Wayne Coulson, contributor
Harold Davis, basketball, 1925-28
Ted Dean, football, 1956-60
Rick Dvorak, football, 1970-74
Cal Elmore, track-cross country, 1961-65
Pike Gawthrop, football, 1937-39
Al Gebert, football coach, 1930-41
Theodore Gore, at-large
Dorothy Harmon, administrator
Don Heinkel, baseball, 1979-82
Ron Heller, basketball, 1958-61
William Hennigh, basketball, 1930-32
Jim Hershberger, at-large
Strong Hinman, football, 1912-17
Anton Houlik, football, 1946-49
Warren (Armstrong) Jabali, basketball, 1965-68
Francis Johnson, basketball-football-track, 1931-34
Gene Johnson, basketball coach, 1928-33
Lynbert Johnson, basketball, 1976-79
Cecil Jordan, football, 1915-18
Marguerite Keeley, basketball, 1975-77
Mike Kennedy, at-large
Jim Klisanin, football-baseball-basketball, 1954-57
Eddie Kriwiel, football, 1947-50
Roland Lakes, football, 1957-61
Cliff Levingston, basketball, 1979-82
The Levitt Family, at-large

Al Littleton, golf, 1947-50, coach 1973-82, 1989-95
Cleo Littleton, basketball, 1951-55
Don Lock, basketball-baseball, 1954-58
Bob Long, football-basketball, 1959-64
Connie Long, track, 1985-89
Harold Manning, track, 1928-31
Ross McBurney, basketball, 1926-29
Xavier McDaniel, basketball, 1981-85
Prince McJunkins, football, 1979-82
Ralph Miller, basketball coach, 1951-64
Russ Morman, baseball, 1982-83
Ray Morrison, football, 1946-50
Gary Navarro, golf, 1969-73
Lester Needham, trainer, 1945-58
Rod Nuckolls, golf, 1977-80
Jimmy Nutter, football, 1947-51
Charlie O'Brien, baseball, 1980-82
Dick Price, golf, 1934-38
Tom Reeves, trainer, 1962-70
Harold Reynolds, basketball, 1924-28
Dick Sanders, baseball-football-basketball, 1950-52
Henry Schichtle, football, 1960-64
Linwood Sexton, football, 1944-48
Robert Shadoan, football, 1929-32
Aubrey Sherrod, basketball, 1981-85
Randy Smith, track-cross country, 1971-75
Erik Sonberg, baseball, 1981-83
Dave Stallworth, basketball, 1962-65
Mark Standiford, baseball, 1985-88
Phil Stephenson, baseball, 1979-82
Johnny Stevens, golf, 1960-64
Lyle Sturdy, football-track, 1940-43
Jamie Thompson, basketball, 1964-67
Lanny Van Eman, basketball-baseball, 1958-62
Paul Vermillion, football, 1923-26
Alan Walker, track, 1969-73
Dwane Wallace, at-large
Jim Waskiewicz, football, 1963-65
Mervyn Webster, tennis, 1968-72
Gene Wiley, basketball, 1959-62

BASEBALL

SEASON BY SEASON HISTORY

Year	Overall			Conference				
	W	L	T	W	L	Finish	Coach	Postseason
1899	0	1					Harry Hess	
1900 record not available							Harry Hess	
1901	7	4					Harry Hess	
1902	8	4					C.P. Clark	
1903	8	6					student coaches	
1904	8	2					Walter Frantz	
1905	9	6	2				A.F. Holste	
1906	9	6					Willis Bates	
1907	8	9					Willis Bates	
1908	8	4					Willis Bates	
1909	4	5					Roy Thomas	

Year	Overall W	Overall L	Conference T	Conference W	Conference L	Finish	Coach	Postseason
1910	0	6						
1911	7	5						
1912	12	3	1					
1913	2	12					E. Van Long	
1914	12	7					Willis Bates	
1915	1	5	1				Harry Buck	
1916	2	4					Harry Buck	
1917	1	2					Lamar Hoover	
1918	1	0					Lamar Hoover	
1919	1	0					Lamar Hoover	
1920-21 no team								
1922 record not available								
1923 record not available								
1924-47 no team								
1948	4	4					Lyle Sturdy	
1949	4	9		0	5	3rd (W)	Ken Gunning	
1950	4	14		1	5	4th (W)	Ken Gunning	
1951	4	9		1	5	4th (W)	Ken Gunning	
1952	3	10		0	6	3rd (S)	Dick Miller	
1953	1	9		0	6	6th	Dick Miller	
1954	4	9		2	7	5th	Forest Jensen	
1955	4	9		3	6	t6th	Forest Jensen	
1956	4	13		1	8	t7th	Jerry Bupp	
1957	7	12		2	7	t6th	Ray Morrison	
1958	17	8		2	4	t2nd (W)	Ray Morrison	
1959	15	12		2	4	3rd (W)	Ray Morrison	
1960	15	12		3	2	2nd (W)	Ray Morrison	
1961	9	7		0	4	2nd (W)	Dick Miller	
1962-63 no team								
1964	8	10		0	4		Lanny Van Eman	
1965	7	13		4	5	t2nd (W)	Verlyn Anderson	
1966	10	8	1	4	2	t1st (W)	Verlyn Anderson	
1967	11	13		2	4	3rd (W)	Verlyn Anderson	
1968	16	8		5	3	2nd (W)	Verlyn Anderson	
1969	17	12		6	3	2nd (W)	Verlyn Anderson	
1970	6	17		3	5	3rd (W)	Verlyn Anderson	
1971-77 no team								
1978	43	30	1				Gene Stephenson	
1979	65	15		10	2		Gene Stephenson	
1980	53	12	1	7	1		Gene Stephenson	MVC Tournament Champion, NCAA Midwest Regional
1981	56	15		15	1	1st (W)	Gene Stephenson	NCAA Atlantic Regional
1982	73	14		15	1	1st (W)	Gene Stephenson	MVC Tournament Champion, College World Series Runnerup
1983	55	18		7	1	1st (W)	Gene Stephenson	NCAA Midwest Regional
1984	40	22		7	7	4th	Gene Stephenson	
1985	68	20		15	5	1st	Gene Stephenson	MVC Tournament Champion, NCAA Midwest Regional
1986	45	18		12	8	2nd	Gene Stephenson	
1987	59	20		13	7	1st	Gene Stephenson	MVC Tournament Champion, NCAA West I Regional
1988	56	16	1	16	4	1st	Gene Stephenson	MVC Tournament Champion, College World Series (T3rd)
1989	68	16		13	5	1st	Gene Stephenson	National Champion
1990	45	19		14	6	t1st	Gene Stephenson	NCAA Midwest Regional
1991	66	13		21	13	1st	Gene Stephenson	MVC Tournament Champion, College World Series Runnerup
1992	56	11		18	3	1st	Gene Stephenson	MVC Tournament Champion, College World Series (0-2)
1993	58	17		17	3	1st	Gene Stephenson	MVC Tournament Champion, College World Series Runnerup
1994	45	17		19	2	1st	Gene Stephenson	NCAA Midwest Regional
1995	53	17		24	8	1st	Gene Stephenson	NCAA Midwest I Regional
Total	1,272	619	8					

MVC CHAMPIONSHIPS

1966, 1981, 1982, 1983, 1985, 1987, 1988, 1989, 1990, 1991, 1992, 1993, 1994, 1995

MVC TOURNAMENT CHAMPIONSHIPS

1980, 1982, 1985, 1987, 1988, 1991, 1992, 1993

TOURNAMENT RECORDS

MVC Tournament Record – 44-20-1 (.688)
NCAA Tournament Record – 47-26 (.644)

BASEBALL POSTSEASON AWARDS

NCAA COACH OF THE YEAR

1982 Gene Stephenson (All-America Baseball News)
1989 Gene Stephenson (The Sporting News, ABCA)
1993 Gene Stephenson (Baseball America)

MVC COACH OF THE YEAR

Gene Stephenson (1980, 1981, 1982, 1985, 1987, 1988, 1989, 1991, 1992, 1994)

NCAA PLAYER OF THE YEAR

1981 Joe Carter (The Sporting News, All-America Baseball News)
1982 Phil Stephenson (All-America Baseball News)
1993 Darren Dreifort (R.E. `Bob' Smith Award)

GOLDEN SPIKES AWARD

1993 Darren Dreifort

FIRST TEAM ALL-AMERICANS

1979 Joe Carter	1987 Tim Raley
1980 Joe Carter	1988 Mark Standiford
1981 Joe Carter	1989 Eric Wedge
1981 Phil Stephenson	1991 Kennie Steenstra
1982 Phil Stephenson	1991 Billy Hall
1982 Don Heinkel	1992 Darren Dreifort
1982 Charlie O'Brien	1993 Darren Dreifort
1982 Bryan Oelkers	1994 Shane Dennis
1983 Russ Morman	

NATIONAL ACADEMIC ATHLETE OF THE YEAR

1992 Charlie Giaudrone

FIRST TEAM ACADEMIC ALL-AMERICANS

1982 Don Heinkel	1991 Kennie Steenstra
1983 Tim Gaskell	1992 Charlie Giaudrone
1990 Jeff Bluma	

FIRST-TEAM FRESHMAN ALL-AMERICANS

1984 Tim Raley	1991 Darren Dreifort
1985 David Haas	1992 Richie Taylor
1989 Darrin Paxton	1993 Casey Blake

MVC PLAYER OF THE YEAR

1980 Joe Carter	1985 Ken Greenwood
1981 Joe Carter	1987 Tim Raley
1982 Phil Stephenson	1989 Eric Wedge
1983 Russ Morman	1994 Carl Hall

NCAA PITCHER OF THE YEAR

1982 Bryan Oelkers (All-America Baseball News)

MVC PITCHER OF THE YEAR

1988 David Haas	1993 Darren Dreifort
1989 Greg Brummett	1994 Shane Dennis
1991 Kennie Steenstra	

FIRST TEAM ALL-MISSOURI VALLEY (SINCE 1978)

1978 Bob Bomerito, 3B; Rob Burgess, P; Larry Groves, P-DH; Matt Yeager, OF
1979 Joe Carter, OF; Mike Davis, 3B; Dave Howard, OF
1980 Bob Bomerito, 3B; Joe Carter, OF; Mike Davis, 3B; Terry Hayes, P; Don Heinkel, P; Phil Stephenson, 1B; Jim Thomas, 2B
1981 Joe Carter, OF; Terry Hayes, P; Don Heinkel, P; Phil Stephenson, 1B
1982 Don Heinkel, P; Russ Morman, DH; Charlie O'Brien, C; Bryan Oelkers, P; Phil Stephenson, 1B; Jim Thomas, 2B
1983 Dave Lucas, SS; Russ Morman, 1B; Kevin Penner, OF; Erik Sonberg, P; Jim Spring, 2B
1984 Arnie Beyeler, SS; Loren Hibbs, OF; Greg LaFever, P
1985 Arnie Beyeler, SS; Ken Greenwood, P; Dan Juenke, 1B; Kevin Penner, OF
1986 Arnie Beyeler, SS; Shane Durham, P; David Haas, P; Tim Raley, OF; Mark Standiford, 2B
1987 David Haas, P; Rick Olivas, DH; Tim Raley, OF
1988 David Haas, P; Dan Raley, 1B; Mark Standiford, 2B
1989 Greg Brummett, P; Mike Lansing, SS; Mike McDonald, OF; Eric Wedge, C
1990 Pat Meares, 3B; Doug Mirabelli, C; Chris Wimmer, LF; Kennie Steenstra, P
1991 Billy Hall, 2B; Doug Mirabelli, C; Jason White, 1B; Chris Wimmer, SS
1992 Darren Dreifort, P; Todd Dreifort, OF; Charlie Giaudrone, P; Scot McCloughan, DH; Doug Mirabelli, C; Jason White, 1B; Chris Wimmer, SS
1993 Jaime Bluma, P; Darren Dreifort, P; Joey Jackson, 2B; Toby Smith, 1B; Richie Taylor, OF
1994 Jason Adams, SS; Brandon Baird, P; Casey Blake, 3B; Jaime Bluma, P; Shane Dennis, P; Joey Jackson, 2B
1995 Jason Adams, SS; Brandon Baird, P; Casey Blake, 3B; Mike Drumright, P; Braden Looper, P; Travis Wyckoff, P

MEN'S BASKETBALL

Year	Season W	Season L	Conference W	Conference L	Finish	Coach
1905-06	2	4				Willis Bates
1906-07	3	6				Willis Bates
1907-08	2	3	0	3		Willis Bates
1908-09	4	6	1	2		None
1909-10	3	10	1	7		Roy Thomas
1910-11	7	6	4	6		Roy Thomas
1911-12	2	8	0	8		Roy Thomas
1912-13	1	11	0	10		E.V. Long
1913-14	8	7	4	6		Willis Bates
1914-15	4	10	2	10		Harry Buck
1915-16	10	5	8	5		Harry Buck
1916-17	2	11	1	11		Lamar Hoover
1917-18	3	10				Lamar Hoover
1918-19	1	7				None
1919-20	8	8	6	8		Kenneth Cassidy
1920-21	16	2	15	2	1st	Wilmer Elfrink
1921-22	12	4	9	2	2nd	Lamar Hoover
1922-23	13	7	8	5		Lamar Hoover
1923-24	10	12	8	8		Sam Hill
1924-25	9	9	6	8	11th	Sam Hill
1925-26	14	6	11	4	5th	Leonard Umnus
1926-27	19	2	11	1	2nd	Leonard Umnus
1927-28	14	6	8	4	3rd	Leonard Umnus
1928-29	16	6	9	3	2nd	Gene Johnson
1929-30	14	4	9	3	2nd	Gene Johnson
1930-31	18	5	9	3	2nd	Gene Johnson
1931-32	12	7	7	5	3rd	Gene Johnson
1932-33	14	2	10	2	t1st	Gene Johnson
1933-34 Suspended by North Central Association						
1934-35	7	13	4	4	t3rd	Lindsay Austin
1935-36	12	12	8	8	t3rd	Bill Hennigh
1936-37	9	12	5	5	4th	Bill Hennigh
1937-38	10	13	5	7	t3rd	Bill Hennigh
1938-39	9	12	3	7	5th	Bill Hennigh
1939-40	10	8	5	5	4th	Bill Hennigh
1940-41	9	11				Bill Hennigh
1941-42	4	16				Jack Starrett
1942-43	12	7				Mel Binford
1943-44 No team due to World War II						
1944-45	14	6				Mel Binford
1945-46	14	9	6	4	2nd	Mel Binford
1946-47	8	17	2	10	7th	Mel Binford
1947-48	12	13	1	9	6th	Mel Binford
1948-49	10	16	3	5	5th	Ken Gunning
1949-50	7	17	1	11	7th	Ken Gunning
1950-51	9	16	5	9	5th	Ken Gunning
1951-52	11	19	2	8	6th	Ralph Miller
1952-53	16	11	3	7	6th	Ralph Miller
1953-54	27	4	8	2	2nd	Ralph Miller
1954-55	17	9	4	6	4th	Ralph Miller
1955-56	14	12	6	8	5th	Ralph Miller
1956-57	15	11	8	6	t3rd	Ralph Miller
1957-58	14	12	6	8	5th	Ralph Miller
1958-59	14	12	7	7	4th	Ralph Miller
1959-60	14	12	6	8	t4th	Ralph Miller
1960-61	18	8	6	6	5th	Ralph Miller
1961-62	18	9	7	5	3rd	Ralph Miller
1962-63	19	8	7	5	2nd	Ralph Miller
1963-64	23	6	10	2	t1st	Ralph Miller
1964-65	21	9	11	3	1st	Gary Thompson
1965-66	17	10	9	5	t2nd	Gary Thompson
1966-67	14	12	9	5	3rd	Gary Thompson
1967-68	12	14	7	9	6th	Gary Thompson
1968-69	11	15	7	9	t6th	Gary Thompson
1969-70	8	18	3	13	8th	Gary Thompson
1970-71	10	16	3	11	8th	Gary Thompson
1971-72	16	10	6	8	5th	Harry Miller
1972-73	10	16	6	8	t5th	Harry Miller
1973-74	11	15	6	7	5th	Harry Miller
1974-75	11	15	6	8	5th	Harry Miller
1975-76	18	10	10	2	1st	Harry Miller
1976-77	10	10	7	5	t3rd	Harry Miller
1977-78	13	14	8	8	t5th	Harry Miller
1978-79	14	14	8	8	t3rd	Gene Smithson
1979-80	17	12	9	7	t2nd	Gene Smithson
1980-81	26	7	12	4	1st	Gene Smithson
1981-82	23	6	12	4	t2nd	Gene Smithson
1982-83	25	3	17	1	1st	Gene Smithson
1983-84	18	12	11	5	3rd	Gene Smithson
1984-85	18	13	11	5	t2nd	Gene Smithson
1985-86	14	14	7	9	t5th	Gene Smithson
1986-87	22	11	9	5	3rd	Eddie Fogler
1987-88	20	10	11	3	2nd	Eddie Fogler
1988-89	19	11	10	4	t2nd	Eddie Fogler
1989-90	10	19	6	8	t5th	Mike Cohen
1990-91	14	17	7	9	6th	Mike Cohen
1991-92	8	20	6	12	t7th	Mike Cohen
1992-93	10	17	7	11	t7th	Scott Thompson
1993-94	9	18	6	12	t7th	Scott Thompson
1994-95	13	14	6	12	t8th	Scott Thompson
Totals	1,087	917	539	503		

MVC CHAMPIONSHIPS
1963-64, 1964-65, 1975-76, 1980-81, 1982-83

MVC TOURNAMENT CHAMPIONS
1985, 1987

NCAA TOURNAMENT APPEARANCES
1964, 1965, 1976, 1981, 1985, 1987, 1988

NIT APPEARANCES
1954, 1962, 1963, 1966, 1980, 1984, 1989

TOURNAMENT RECORDS
MVC Tournament record – 13-14
NCAA Tournament record – 6-8
NIT record – 1-7

BASKETBALL POSTSEASON AWARDS

ALL-AMERICANS
1954 Cleo Littleton (Helms Foundation)
1955 Cleo Littleton (3rd team, Helms Foundation)
1964 Dave Stallworth; 1st team, Associated Press, 1st team, United Press International, 1st team, U.S. Basketball Writers, 1st team, The Sporting News
1965 Dave Stallworth; 2nd team, Associated Press
1983 Antoine Carr; 1st team, The Sporting News, 3rd team, Associated Press
1985 Xavier McDaniel; 1st team, Associated Press, 1st team, U.S. Basketball Writers, 2nd team, United Press International, 3rd team, NABC

ACADEMIC ALL-AMERICANS
1967 Jamie Thompson, 1st team
1969 Ron Mendell, 1st team

MVC COACH OF THE YEAR
1955 Ralph Miller   1987 Eddie Fogler
1965 Gary Thompson

MVC PLAYER OF THE YEAR
1983 Antoine Carr   1985 Xavier McDaniel
1984 Xavier McDaniel

Year	
1952	Cleo Littleton
1953	Cleo Littleton
1954	Cleo Littleton
1955	Cleo Littleton
1957	Joe Stevens
1961	Ron Heller, Lanny Van Eman, Gene Wiley
1962	Gene Wiley
1963	Dave Stallworth
1964	Dave Stallworth
1965	Dave Leach, Kelly Pete, Dave Stallworth
1966	Warren Armstrong, Jamie Thompson
1967	Warren Armstrong, Jamie Thompson
1968	Warren Armstrong
1969	Greg Carney
1970	Greg Carney
1971	Terry Benton
1972	Terry Benton
1973	Rich Morsden, Bob Wilson
1975	Robert Elmore
1976	Robert Elmore
1977	Robert Elmore, Cheese Johnson
1978	Cheese Johnson
1979	Cheese Johnson
1981	Cliff Levingston
1982	Antoine Carr, Cliff Levingston
1983	Antoine Carr, Xavier McDaniel
1984	Xavier McDaniel
1985	Xavier McDaniel
1988	Sasha Radunovich
1989	Steve Grayer

1,000-POINT CLUB

Player	Years	Ht.	Hometown	Points	Avg.
1. Cleo Littleton	1951-55	6-3	Wichita (East)	2,164	19.0
2. Xavier McDaniel	1981-85	6-7	Columbia, S.C.	2,152	18.4
3. Dave Stallworth	1962-65	6-7	Dallas	1,936	24.2
4. Antoine Carr	1979-83	6-9	Wichita (Heights)	1,911	17.1
5. Cheese Johnson	1975-79	6-5	New York	1,907	17.3
6. Aubrey Sherrod	1981-85	6-2	Wichita (Heights)	1,765	15.1
7. Greg Carney	1967-70	5-9	Chicago	1,545	20.1
8. Cliff Levingston	1979-82	6-8	San Diego	1,471	16.2
9. Sasha Radunovich	1985-89	6-10	Titograd, Yugoslavia	1,463	12.2
10. Jamie Thompson	1964-67	6-3	Wichita (East)	1,359	17.6
11. Ron Harris	1969-72	6-6	Pittsburgh	1,322	16.9
12. Warren Armstrong	1965-68	6-2	Kansas City, Mo.	1,301	16.7
13. Joe Stevens	1955-58	5-11	Wichita (North)	1,295	16.6
14. Gus Santos	1983-87	6-7	New York	1,278	11.5
15. Paul Guffrovich	1987-91	6-3	Nanticoke, Pa.	1,247	12.2
16. Steve Grayer	1985-89	6-8	Macon, Ga.	1,221	10.2
17. Robert Elmore	1973-77	6-10	Jamaica, N.Y.	1,186	14.1
18. Calvin Bruton	1972-76	5-9	New York	1,184	11.6
19. Kelly Pete	1963-66	6-1	Wichita (East)	1,169	14.1
20. Vince Smith	1970-73	6-5	St. Louis	1,163	15.1
21. John Cooper	1987-91	6-6	Kansas City, Mo.	1,153	11.9
22. Al Tate	1957-60	6-4	Coffeyville	1,139	14.6
23. Bob Hodgson	1953-56	6-6	Scammon	1,122	13.7
24. Lanny Van Eman	1958-62	5-11	McKeesport, Pa.	1,119	14.0
25. Ernie Moore	1960-64	5-10	Kansas City, Kan.	1,055	13.2
26. Bob Trogele	1975-79	6-3	Somers, N.Y.	1,028	9.3
27. Ron Heller	1958-61	6-6	McKeesport, Pa.	1,022	13.1
28. Ron Washington	1965-69	6-5	Chicago	1,013	14.7
29. Terry Benton	1969-72	6-8	Wichita (East)	1,003	13.2

WOMEN'S BASKETBALL

1985 Jenny Parr, 3rd team

MVC PLAYER OF THE YEAR

1991-92 Kareema Williams

FIRST-TEAM ALL-MVC OR ALL-GATEWAY

1982-83 Lisa Hodgson
1983-84 Lisa Hodgson
1984-85 Allison Daniel
1985-86 Allison Daniel
1991-92 Kareema Williams
1992-93 Ann Hollingsworth
1993-94 Kim Evans, Ann Hollingsworth
1994-95 Kim Evans

SEASON BY SEASON HISTORY

Year	Overall W	Overall L	Conference W	Conference L	Finish	Coach
1974-75	4	13				Larry Thye
1975-76	11	6				Larry Thye
1976-77	11	17				Larry Thye
1977-78	6	20				Larry Thye
1978-79	6	20				Kathryn Bunnell
1979-80	14	13				Kathryn Bunnell
1980-81	20	11				Kathryn Bunnell
1981-82	15	17				Kathryn Bunnell
1982-83	16	12				Kathryn Bunnell
1983-84	14	14	12	6	4th	Karen Harden
1984-85	10	18	6	12	8th	Karen Harden
1985-86	12	15	9	9	6th	Karen Harden
1986-87	12	14	5	13	8th	Karen Harden
1987-88	9	17	6	12	t6th	Karen Harden
1988-89	6	20	4	14	t9th	Karen Harden
1989-90	7	20	6	12	7th	Linda Hargrove
1990-91	6	21	3	15	9th	Linda Hargrove
1991-92	13	16	10	8	5th	Linda Hargrove
1992-93	15	12	8	8	t4th	Linda Hargrove
1993-94	17	10	9	7	t3rd	Linda Hargrove
1994-95	16	12	11	7	5th	Linda Hargrove
Totals	240	318				

FOOTBALL

MVC CHAMPIONSHIPS
1954, 1955, 1960, 1961, 1963

BOWL APPEARANCES
Raisin Bowl, 1/1/48; Camelia Bowl, 12/30/48;
Sun Bowl, 12/27/61

FOOTBALL POSTSEASON AWARDS

MVC COACH OF THE YEAR

1954	Jack Mitchell	1961	Hank Foldberg
1960	Hank Foldberg	1963	Chelo Huerta

MVC OFFENSIVE PLAYER OF THE YEAR
1981 Prince McJunkins, QB
1982 Prince McJunkins, QB

MVC DEFENSIVE PLAYER OF THE YEAR
1978 Brian Anderson, LB

MVC NEWCOMER OF THE YEAR
1971 Rick Dvorak, DT
1977 Mickey Collins, RB
1979 Prince McJunkins, QB
1980 Rueben Eckels, FL
1982 Eric Denson, TB

FIRST-TEAM ALL-MISSOURI VALLEY (1945-84)
1945 Linwood Sexton, HB
1946 Linwood Sexton, HB
1947 Art Hodges, FB; Paul Houser, T; Linwood
Sexton, HB
1949 Jimmy Nutter, HB
1954 Jack Conway, QB; Ralph Denton, G; Darrell
Hill, T; Leroy Hinman, FB; Jim Klisanin, HB;
Jack O'Toole, C; Neil Sikes, E
1955 Jim Klisanin, HB; Jack O'Toole, C; Vere
Wellman, T
1956 Jim Herlocker, G; Jim Klisanin, HB
1958 Ted Dean, FB
1959 Ted Dean, FB; Roland Lakes, C; Ray Wichert, E

1960 Roland Lakes, C; Willie Mallory, HB; Nelson
Toburen, E
1961 Leroy Leep, C; Jim Maddox, E; Ron Turner, E;
Alex Zyskowski, QB
1962 Miller Farr, HB; Jim Maddox, E; Charles
Wright, G
1963 Henry Schichtle, QB; Jim Waskiewicz, C
1964 Pete DiDonato, FB
1965 Pete DiDonato, FB; Jim Waskiewicz, LB
1966 John Eckman, QB; Jimmie Jones, DE; Glenn
Meltzer, E
1967 Jimmie Jones, DE
1968 Bob Johnson, LB; Pete Robertson, TB
1969 Lynn Duncan, DT
1970 Rick Dvorak, DT; Randy Jackson, FB; Lino
Venerucci, LB
1972 Rick Dvorak, DT; John Potts, K; Lino
Venerucci, LB
1973 Rick Dvorak, DT
1974 Dave Warren, LB
1975 Dave Crandell, NG; Dave Warren, LB
1976 Barry Bales, OL; Alvin Brooks, CB; Leon
Dobbs, SE; Clem Jankowski, NG; Ron
Shumon, LB
1977 Jim Andrus, QB; Barry Bales, OL; Bryan
Hanning, SE; Clem Jankowski, NG; Ron
Shumon, LB; Willie Smith, DE; Sherman
Taylor, CB; Ted Vincent, DT
1978 Barry Bales, OL; Willie Smith, DE; Brian
Anderson, LB
1979 Brian Anderson, LB; Rodney Woods, DL
1980 Mickey Collins, RB; David Davis, DL; Mark
McCoy, OL; Kurt Vestman, TE; Billy Wilson, DB
1981 Prince McJunkins, QB; Bobby Weston, DT;
Curtis Whitten, SS
1982 Reuben Eckels, WR; Jay Hull, OL; Lonnie
Kennell, DL; Prince McJunkins, QB; Glen
Stewart, DB
1983 Greg Blackman, OL; Eric Denson, RB; Anthony
Jones, TE
1984 Maurice Foxworth, DB

Year	W	L	T	Coach
1897	1	0		T.H. Morrison
1898	0	1		Student coaches
1899	2	1	2	Harry Hess
1900	5	3		Harry Hess
1901	3	6		Harry Hess
1902	4	3	1	Guy Peverly
1903	6	2		Student coaches
1904	5	4		A.F. Holste
1905	5	4	1	Willis Bates
1906	7	1	2	Willis Bates
1907	8	2		Willis Bates
1908	8	1		Willis Bates
1909	2	5	1	Roy Thomas
1910	6	2	1	Roy Thomas
1911	7	1		Roy Thomas
1912	4	5		E.V. Long
1913	2	6		E.V. Long
1914	2	3	2	Harry Buck
1915	3	5	1	Harry Buck
1916	7	3		Lamar Hoover
1917	3	3	2	Lamar Hoover
1918	1	4		J.L. Banbury
1919	1	5	2	Kenneth Cassidy
1920	2	3		W.D. Elfrink
1921	5	2	1	Lamar Hoover
1922	3	6	1	Lamar Hoover
1923	2	4	2	Sam Hill
1924	6	2	1	Sam Hill
1925	3	1	4	Leonard Umnus
1926	6	2		Leonard Umnus
1927	3	4		Leonard Umnus
1928	3	5		Sam Hill
1929	3	3	2	Sam Hill
1930	6	3	1	Al Gebert
1931	7	3		Al Gebert
1932	7	2		Al Gebert
1933	8	2		Al Gebert
1934	5	3	1	Al Gebert
1935	5	4		Al Gebert
1936	4	5		Al Gebert
1937	7	3		Al Gebert
1938	7	2	1	Al Gebert
1939	5	3	2	Al Gebert
1940	6	4		Al Gebert
1941	1	6	1	Al Gebert
1942	5	4		Ralph Graham
1943	No games played due to World War II			
1944	5	2	1	Mel Binford
1945	6	4		Mel Binford
1946	5	5		Ralph Graham
1947	7	4		Ralph Graham
1948	5	4	1	Jim Trimble
1949	3	6	1	Jim Trimble
1950	5	4	1	Jim Trimble
1951	2	7		Bob Carlson
1952	3	6	1	Bob Carlson
1953	4	4	1	Jack Mitchell
1954	9	1		Jack Mitchell
1955	7	2	1	Pete Tillman
1956	4	6		Pete Tillman
1957	1	9		Chalmer Woodard
1958	4	5	1	Chalmer Woodard
1959	5	4	1	Chalmer Woodard
1960	8	2		Hank Foldberg
1961	8	3		Hank Foldberg
1962	3	7		Chelo Huerta
1963	7	2		Chelo Huerta
1964	4	6		Chelo Huerta
1965	2	7		George Karras
1966	2	8		George Karras
1967	2	7	1	Boyd Converse
1968	0	10	0	Eddie Kriwiel
1969	2	8		Ben Wilson
1970	0	9		Ben Wilson, Bob Seaman
1971	3	8		Bob Seaman
1972	6	5		Bob Seaman
1973	4	7		Bob Seaman
1974	1	9	1	Jim Wright
1975	3	8		Jim Wright
1976	4	7		Jim Wright
1977	5	6		Jim Wright
1978	4	7		Jim Wright
1979	1	10		Willie Jeffries
1980	5	5	1	Willie Jeffries
1981	4	6	1	Willie Jeffries
1982	8	3		Willie Jeffries
1983	3	8		Willie Jeffries
1984	2	9		Ron Chismar
1985	3	8		Ron Chismar
1986	3	8		Ron Chismar
Totals	375	402	47	

MEN'S CROSS COUNTRY

NCAA CHAMPIONSHIP MEETS

Year	Coach	Placing
1965	Fritz Snodgrass	DNP
1971	Herm Wilson	14th
1973	Herm Wilson	18th
1974	Herm Wilson	17th
1975	Herm Wilson	26th

MVC CHAMPIONSHIP TEAMS

1960, 1961, 1971, 1972, 1973, 1974, 1975, 1987

NCAA ALL-AMERICANS

Year	Athlete, Event	Placing
1972	Alan Walker, 6 miles (29:22.0)	22nd
1974	Randy Smith, 6 miles (30:11.1)	10th
1982	George Collier, 10,000 meters (30:55.6)	27th
1990	Mornay Annandale, 10,000 meters (29:55.0)	17th
1992	Mornay Annandale, 10,000 meters (31:30.4)	19th

MVC INDIVIDUAL CHAMPIONS

Year	Athlete	Event	Time
1961	Carl Elmore	3 miles	15:54
1962	Carl Elmore	3 miles	14:57
1967	Roy Old Person	4 miles	19:46.7
1972	Alan Walker	5 miles	24:52.5
1973	Randy Smith	5 miles	25:34.4
1974	Randy Smith	5 miles	24:41.5
1982	George Collier	5 miles	24:58.8
1987	Trey Harrison	8000 meters	24:32.82
1990	Mornay Annandale	8000 meters	24:35
1991	Mornay Annandale	8000 meters	24:58.16
1992	Mornay Annandale	8000 meters	24:04

WOMEN'S CROSS COUNTRY

GATEWAY CHAMPIONSHIP TEAMS

1987, 1988, 1990

GATEWAY INDIVIDUAL CHAMPIONS

Year	Athlete	Event	Time
1983	Susan Hammock	5000 meters	16:56.24

MEN'S GOLF

NCAA CHAMPIONSHIP APPEARANCES, INDIVIDUAL

Year	Player	Site	Finish
1949	Al Littleton	Ames, Iowa	t17th
1962	John Stevens	Durham, N.C.	t33rd
1963	John Stevens	Wichita C.C.	t17th
1964	John Stevens	Broadmoor, Colo.	cut
1972	Gary Navarro	Cape Coral, Fla.	cut
1973	Gary Navarro	Stillwater, Okla.	na
1976	Don Lee	Albuquerque	cut
1978	Rod Nuckolls	Eugene, Ore.	t23rd
1980	Rod Nuckolls	Columbus, Ohio	cut

NCAA CHAMPIONSHIP APPEARANCES, TEAM

Year	Site	Finish
1974	Santee, Calif.	cut
1977	Hamilton, N.Y.	22nd
1978	Eugene, Ore.	19th
1979	Winston-Salem, N.C.	25th
1994	Oklahoma City	21st

MISSOURI VALLEY CONFERENCE CHAMPIONSHIPS

Year	Player	Site	Score
1954	Sam Sadler	NA	215
1962	John Stevens	Peoria, Ill.	212
1964	John Stevens	Louisville, Ky.	215
1972	Gary Navarro	Memphis, Tenn.	214
1977	Mike Caster	Wichita St. G.C.	282
1980	Rod Nuckolls	Terre Haute, Ind.	296
1986	Doug Brenneman	Pekin, Ill.	303
1989	Jon Platz	Normal, Ill.	301

MISSOURI VALLEY CONFERENCE CHAMPIONSHIPS, TEAM

Year	Site
1946	NA
1977	Wichita St. G.C.
1978	Peoria, Ill.
1979	Des Moines
1984	Wichita St. G.C.
1986	Pekin, Ill.

WOMEN'S GOLF

SCORING RECORDS

NCAA CHAMPIONSHIP APPEARANCES

Year	Player	Site	Finish	Scores
1993	Clara Rodriguez	Tucson	t71st	77-77-76=230
1994	Clara Rodriguez	Albuquerque	t80th	80-82-78=240

MISSOURI VALLEY CONFERENCE CHAMPIONSHIPS, INDIVIDUAL

Year	Player	Site	Scores
1987	Ann Vandermillen	WSU Course	78-78-82=242

MISSOURI VALLEY CONFERENCE CHAMPIONSHIPS, TEAM

Year	Site	Scores
1987	WSU Golf Course	329-324-352=1005
1992	Tallgrass Country Club	328-317-333=978

SOFTBALL

GATEWAY ALL-DECADE TEAM
Patty Bautista, P (1986-89)

GATEWAY CONFERENCE MVP
1989 Patty Bautista, P

ACADEMIC ALL-AMERICA
1988 Shannah Biggan, 3B, 1st team
1990 Debra Loehr, DH, 3rd team

GATEWAY NEWCOMER OF THE YEAR
1984 Lora Heit, SS

ALL-GATEWAY, ALL-MISSOURI VALLEY
1987 Patty Bautista, Utility, 1st team
1989 Patty Bautista, P, 1st team
1991 Lorie Broehl, C, 1st team; Jennifer Jay, Utility, 1st team
1992 Lorie Broehl, C, 1st team; Kristin Klumpp, OF, 1st team
1993 Jennifer Jay, Utility, 1st team; Lorie Broehl, C, 1st team; Nikki Epley, 2B, 2nd team; Kristin Klumpp, OF, 2nd team; Jodie Musser, P, 2nd team
1994 Kristin Klumpp, OF, 2nd team; Bobbie Paull, 3B, 2nd team
1995 Bobbie Paull, 3B, 2nd team; Beth Wilson, P, 2nd team; Stacey hart, P, 2nd team; Jennifer Bachman, 2B, 2nd team; Ozzie Smith, SS, 2nd team; Michelle Moores, Utility, 2nd team

MEN'S TENNIS

NCAA ALL-AMERICANS, SINGLES
1964 Ben Anzola
1983 Roberto Saad

NCAA ALL-AMERICANS, DOUBLES
1983 Roberto Saad-Paul Smith

MISSOURI VALLEY CHAMPIONS, TEAM
1959, 1964, 1965, 1978, 1979, 1980, 1981, 1982, 1983, 1984, 1985, 1986, 1987, 1988, 1989, 1991, 1994

MISSOURI VALLEY CHAMPIONS, SINGLES – NO. 1
1979	Mark McMahon	1984	Dale Houston
1980	Mark McMahon	1987	Jeremy Grubi
1981	Roberto Saad	1991	Darren Frlan
1982	Roberto Saad	1992	Simon Cornish
1983	Roberto Saad	1994	Phil Cooper

MISSOURI VALLEY CHAMPIONS, SINGLES – NO. 2
1978	Myron Pushyk	1985	Jeremy Grubi
1979	Myron Pushyk	1987	Andy Wintrich
1980	Myron Pushyk	1992	Darren Frlan
1982	Paul Smith	1994	Simon Cornish
1983	Paul Smith		

MISSOURI VALLEY CHAMPIONS, SINGLES – NO. 3
1976	Jay Louderback	1984	John Thorpe
1978	Alex Marshall	1985	Kris Braaten
1979	Bill Nichols	1986	Andy Wintrich
1980	Brod Dyke	1987	Stephen Salthouse
1981	Paul Smith	1989	Paul Grubi
1982	Steve Guy	1991	Richard Lamothe
1983	Dale Houston		

MISSOURI VALLEY CHAMPIONS, SINGLES – NO. 4
1978	Bill Nichols	1987	Daniel Aspelin
1982	Par Larsson	1988	Paul Rosenich
1984	Simon Norman	1989	Darren Price
1985	Stephen Salthouse	1990	Peter Swanell
1986	Kris Braaten		

MISSOURI VALLEY CHAMPIONS, SINGLES – NO. 5
1978	Rex Coad	1986	John Thorpe
1980	Bill Nichols	1987	Jan Ernston
1982	Dale Houston	1989	Darren Frlan
1985	Brent Fields	1995	Simon Evelyn

MISSOURI VALLEY CHAMPIONS, SINGLES – NO. 6
1979	Steve Guy	1985	Paul Rosenich
1980	Steve Guy	1987	Darin Weidenheimer
1984	Mike Scherer	1989	Peter Swanell

MISSOURI VALLEY CHAMPIONS, SINGLES – NO. 7
1994	Richard Lamothe	1995	Chad Bohling

MISSOURI VALLEY CHAMPIONS, DOUBLES – NO. 1
1975	Jay Louderback-Doug Glendenning
1979	Brod Dyke-Mark McMahon
1980	Brod Dyke-Mark McMahon
1981	Roberto Saad-Brod Dyke
1982	Paul Smith-Steve Guy
1983	Roberto Saad-Paul Smith
1988	Andrew McLean-Stephen Salthouse
1991	Darren Frlan-Simon Cornish
1994	Simon Cornish-Jason Grubb

MISSOURI VALLEY CHAMPIONS, DOUBLES – NO. 2
1978	Alex Marshall-Myron Pushyk
1979	Bill Nichols-Nigel O'Rourke
1980	Bill Nichols-Nigel O'Rourke
1984	John Thorpe-Dale Houston
1985	Andy Castle-Stephen Salthouse
1986	Stephen Salthouse-John Thorpe
1987	Daniel Aspelin-Stephen Salthouse
1988	Paul Rosenich-Harald Eksandh
1989	Andrew Ritter-Darren Price
1990	Andrew Ritter-Darren Frlan

MISSOURI VALLEY CHAMPIONS, DOUBLES – NO. 3
1979	Myron Pushyk-Steve Guy
1980	Myron Pushyk-Steve Guy
1982	Par Larsson-Simon Norman
1983	Andy Castle-Simon Norman
1984	Kris Braaten-Jeremy Grubi
1986	Kris Braaten-Paul Rosenich
1988	Darin Weidenheimer-Brent Dennison
1992	Simon Cornish-Lance Lechner

WOMEN'S TENNIS

NCAA CHAMPIONSHIP QUALIFIERS, SINGLES
1984 Sandy Sadler

NCAA CHAMPIONSHIP QUALIFIERS, DOUBLES
1984 Sandy Sadler-Jill Braendle
1985 Sandy Sadler-Jill Braendle

GATEWAY/MVC CHAMPIONS, TEAM
1982, 1984, 1986, 1988, 1994, 1995

GATEWAY/MVC CHAMPIONS, SINGLES – NO. 1
1982	Sandy Sadler	1986	Jill Braendle
1983	Sandy Sadler	1990	Karen Theck
1984	Sandy Sadler	1994	Melanie Theck
1985	Sandy Sadler	1995	Lisa Field

GATEWAY/MVC CHAMPIONS, SINGLES – NO. 2
1982 Susan Deam   1985 Jill Braendle
1984 Jill Braendle

GATEWAY/MVC CHAMPIONS, SINGLES – NO. 3
1982 Karen Gibbs   1983 Jill Braendle

GATEWAY/MVC CHAMPIONS, SINGLES – NO. 4
1986 Sally Webber

GATEWAY/MVC CHAMPIONS, SINGLES – NO. 5
1982 Cindy Baker

GATEWAY/MVC CHAMPIONS, SINGLES – NO. 6
1982 Jan Louderback

GATEWAY/MVC CHAMPIONS, DOUBLES – NO. 1
1982 Sandy Sadler-Karen Gibbs
1983 Sandy Sadler-Jill Braendle
1984 Sandy Sadler-Jill Braendle
1985 Sandy Sadler-Jill Braendle

GATEWAY/MVC CHAMPIONS, DOUBLES – NO. 2
1983 Susan Deam-Molly Maine

GATEWAY/MVC CHAMPIONS, DOUBLES – NO. 3
1982 Molly Maine-Cindy Pauls
1984 Gloria Orue-Eiran Swart

MEN'S TRACK AND FIELD

OLYMPIC TEAM MEMBERS
1936	Harold Manning	3000m steeple (5th)
1972	Preston Carrington	Long jump (3rd, 26-2 1/2)
1988	Iziaq Adeyanju*	100m (DNP)

* competed for Nigeria

U.S. OLYMPIC TRIALS PARTICIPANTS
1924	Bill Nicholson	1600m (7th)
1936	Harold Manning	3000m steeple (qualifier)
1960	Lew Merriman	800m (5th, 1:47.9)
1968	Fred Burton	Pole vault (WD)
1972	Alan Walker	1500m (DNP)
1972	Preston Carrington	Long jump (qualifier)
1972	Randy Smith	3000m steeple (DNP)
1976	Randy Smith	3000m steeple (DNP)
1980	Don Duvall	Long jump (12th, 25-2)
1988	Gene Abernathy	Discus (7th, 185-0)
1992	John Hamilton	Hammer (26th, 195-3)

NCAA INDOOR ALL-AMERICANS
1975	Randy Smith	2-mile (3rd, 8:48.6)
1992	John Hamilton	35-lb. weight throw (2nd, 65-11)

NCAA OUTDOOR ALL-AMERICANS
1930	Harold Manning	2-mile (1st)
1959	Lew Merriman	880 yds. (4th)
1963	Cal Elmore	Mile (2nd, 4:02.2)
1967	Fred Burton	Pole vault (2nd, 16-0)
1970	Preston Carrington	Long jump (3rd, 25-9)
1971	Preston Carrington	Long jump (6th, 24-9)
1973	Temoer Terry	High jump (6th, 7-1)
1975	Randy Smith	3000m steeple (2nd)
1978	Don Duvall	Long jump (6th, 25-11 3/4)
1989	Gene Abernathy	Discus (7th, 185-0)
1991	Mornay Annandale	10,000m (6th, 28:48.64)
1991	John Hamilton	Hammer (9th, 205-9)
1995	Einars Tupuritis	800m (8th)

MVC TEAM CHAMPIONSHIPS
1966	69 points	Fritz Snodgrass
1972	138 points	Herm Wilson
1994	172 points	John Kornelson

WOMEN'S TRACK AND FIELD

1992	Connie Long	High jump (DNP)

NCAA INDOOR ALL-AMERICANS

1986	Connie Long	High jump (6th, 5-10 1/4)
1989	Connie Long	High jump (t4th, 5-10)

NCAA OUTDOOR ALL-AMERICANS

1989	Connie Long	High jump (2nd, 6-0 3/4)
1993	Denise Brungardt	Heptathlon (6th, 5,490 pts)
1994	Deana Alexander	Javelin (9th, 166-7)

VOLLEYBALL

ALL-GATEWAY (1983-91), ALL-MVC (1992-)

1986 Becky Wells, 2nd team; Kari James, honorable
     mention
1988 P.J. Barrett, 2nd team
1989 Terri Brown, 2nd team
1990 Terri Brown, 1st team; Yu-Chyi Yang, honor-
     able mention
1991 Janelle Watton, 1st team; Yu-Chyi Yang, 1st
     team
1992 Kristin Carr, 1st team; Kim Henry, 2nd team;
     Kori Rosenkranz, honorable mention
1993 Kristin Carr, 1st team
1995 Angie Hallagin, honorable mention

FRESHMAN OF THE YEAR

1991	Nona Saldana	1992	Kori Rosenkranz

NEWCOMER OF THE YEAR

1988	Karen Nickel	1990	Kristin Carr

QUIZ ANSWERS

1. Wichita State has beaten Drake 69 times and has lost to both Bradley and Southwestern 55 times each.

2. Ralph Miller made $5,000 in his first season.

3. Miller's first assistant was his brother, Dick.

4. Dave Leach, Kelly Pete and Dave Stallworth were first-teamers in 1965.

5. At 7-2, Ron Smith played briefly with the 1970-71 team, and Paul Wight was a reserve on the 1991-92 squad.

6. Warren Armstrong got the nickname "Batman" because of the way he could soar through the air.

7. Cal Bruton was a third-round draft pick of the New York Mets in the 1972 amateur draft.

8. John Kobar was called "The Bionic Man" because of his leaping ability for a 5-foot-9 guard.

9. Roman Welch was the first Gene Smithson signee.

10. Cliff Levingston's high school coach called him "Good News" because he always made good things happen on the court.

11. Rice, led by future NBA guard Ricky Pierce, beat North Carolina State for the '81 Rainbow Classic title.

12. In 1975-76, Cheese Johnson, Robert Elmore, Cal Bruton and Bob Trogele all played together. In 1981-82, those slots were occupied by Cliff Levingston, Antoine Carr, Aubrey Sherrod and Xavier McDaniel. In 1987-88 and 1988-89, the four were Sasha Radunovich, Steve Grayer, Paul Guffrovich and John Cooper.

13. Texas defeated Wake Forest in the championship game.

14. Ron Tyler, who later donated $425,000 toward renovations to Eck Stadium, made the 1966 start.

15. Gymnastics got the axe the same day as baseball.

16. George Wright, from Oklahoma City, never played at WSU. He was drafted and signed with the Texas Rangers out of high school.

17. Bob Bomerito homered in WSU's first game of the '78 season, a loss to Emporia State.

18. In 1980, Terry Hayes pitched 30 2/3 scoreless innings.

19. Creighton beat WSU 5-3 in the finale of a four-game series in Omaha.

20. Jim Thomas, who was called out at third to end the game, was ejected for arguing after the game ended.

21. Kevin Penner's blast onto 21st Street helped WSU beat Kansas Newman 12-2.

22. Mike Drumright fanned 17 Illinois State batters in a 1994 game.

23. None. Every major-league club (excluding Florida and Colorado) has signed at least one Shocker from the Gene Stephenson era.

24. Right fielder Todd Dreifort did not make an error during the 1992 season.

25. Morrison was an assistant librarian.

26. Lucille Ball greeted the Shockers.

27. Jimmy Johnson, who was a coach for one season at WSU before moving on to bigger things.

28. Baseball star Joe Carter led the football Shockers in punt returns with a six-yard average.

29. Roland Lakes played 11 years, James Geathers 10 (entering 1995), Tom Owen nine and Miller Farr nine.

30. Kelley became a member of the Minnesota Fillies.

31. Hargrove was 1-1 against WSU, winning a 1978 game and losing a 1979 game.

32. Al Littleton in 1949 and John Stevens in 1963 both finished in a 17th-place tie at the NCAAs, losing in the second round of match play.

33. The 1994 Shockers had the best combined grade-point average (3.320) of any NCAA softball team.